ISTRIA

ISTRIA

Recipes and stories from the hidden heart
of Italy, Slovenia and Croatia

Paola Bacchia

Smith
Street
Books

CONTENTS

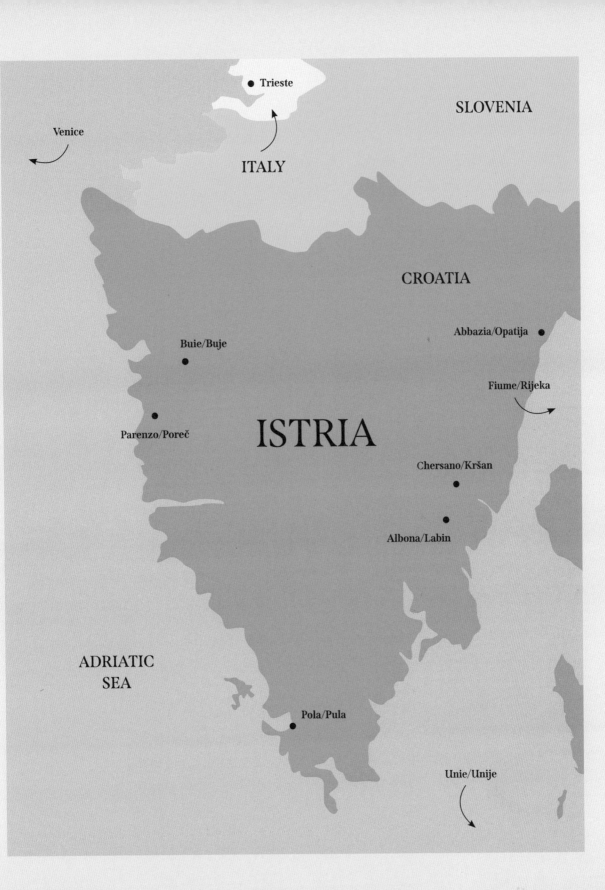

The car pulled up at Karlo's restaurant by the beach at Stoia, just south of Pola. My uncle's friends were waiting for us, and greeted my father like the long-absent brother he was. It had been 24 years since my father Nello had left Istria, and this was his first time back in the town of his birth. As soon as we walked in, we knew what was in the kitchen. The flavours in the air were those of home: mussels on the shell under the grill, garlicky potatoes and Swiss chard on the stovetop, crumbed sardines sizzling in a shallow pool of olive oil. Outside, the water lapped on the wooden dinghies in the bay, gulls squawked, diving into the water in search of fish; inside, a chorus of voices was singing the old folk songs – *canzoni vecie* – in Istrian–Venetian dialect around the lunch table. It was the early 1970s and my first visit to Istria – the place I knew of from stories and photos.

Istria is a promontory at the northern crux of the Adriatic Sea. It is placed like a keystone in the arch of folding hills and valleys where Italy, Slovenia, Austria and Croatia meet. It is all of those countries separately, and an entirely unique country combined. Rows of vines and olive trees grow in its fields of red earth at the foot of towns built from the Istrian stone that emerges from quarries as pale as cream, and becomes honeyed in the tide of time and sun. In August, Istria's coastline surrenders to every delightful cliché of a European summer, while October brings the scent of pine and salt from the forests that meet the sea. And then, in December, Istrians turn their shoulders to the fierce arctic wind known as la Bora. It is the country of my father and it is his lasting gift to me.

In distant Australia, not a day went by that he did not talk about Istria and his *istriani* friends. Over three-quarters of Italian Istrians left in the late 1940s and early 1950s, when most of the peninsula was ceded to Yugoslavia after World War II. His homeland became an obsession: he wrote and received letters, books, photos and newspaper articles from other *istriani*, made plans to join *istriani* reunions in Italy, formed local social clubs, keeping his culture and that of his friends scattered all over the globe alive. Once retired, he discovered the cook Lidia Bastianich, an Italian–Istrian who had migrated to the United States as a child. He taped her TV cooking shows, so he and my mother could replay them, write down the recipes and later recreate the dishes. My mother did the cooking while he enthusiastically prompted her from his perch in our kitchen, using his notes to make sure she followed Lidia's instructions to a tee.

In the post-war period, displaced Europeans were offered free passage to Australia in exchange for two years of work for the government. My parents arrived here by ship on 13 May 1950, travelling with fellow *istriani* Emma, Stanco, Ernesto, Antonietta, Bruno and Elsie. Once in Melbourne, they met Mario, Gemma, Bibo, Jole, Marino, Maria, Silvano and Furio. They sponsored both of my mother's brothers, and their wives, to migrate to Australia and join their expanding community. They worked in factories, on farms, bought land and built houses. They spoke in Istrian–Venetian dialect and gathered in their newly built homes, by the beach and at picnics in the bush, playing card games, drinking home-made wine and sharing the food that connected them to their homeland: sweet *pinza* and *crostoli*, grilled calamari and freshly caught snapper, hearty soups, beans and polenta, home-made gnocchi and pasta, salads with potatoes and home-grown leafy greens – and garlic used liberally, on almost everything.

Food – both eating it and growing it – was central to my father's life. He was houseproud, and when we bought a new house in 1973, he dug out a wine cellar underneath it using a crowbar to break the dense clay. (It took him years, but the storage of wine to an *istriano* was almost as important as the home above it.) He built a double garage, with his workbench and tools occupying one half of it, made bookshelves and tables, wallpapered the walls (and ceiling), and tended to a prolific vegetable garden, growing beans, figs, plums, tomatoes, garlic and the leafy greens – *radiceto* – he had grown up with. Weekends in the home were for working, not relaxing. He would walk into the kitchen at about 11.30 am on Saturdays, wearing his work shorts and a singlet, no matter what season it was, place a hand against the wall and exclaim: '*Livia, da'me de magnar che me trema le gambe!*' ('Livia, prepare some food, my legs are shaking!'). He was, like many Italians, prone to drama and a bit of exaggeration.

My mother learned to cook the dishes he liked. She was born near Treviso, in the region of Veneto. Her family did not cook with garlic, and seafood was a rarity. Once married and in Australia, she learned to cook the Istrian way from the ladies in her social group, mainly to please my father, but she grew to love it too: she started adding garlic to all her savoury dishes, learned to cook a fish *brodetto* (stew), a seafood risotto that she would make for my birthday each year, a hearty bean soup with sauerkraut called *iota*, which my father requested every winter, and was shown by my aunt Alba, who came from Zara, how to make the super-fine stretched pastry for her apple strudel. She would make two strudels in one sitting, as we would invariably eat the first one on the same day it was made.

Istria has Roman ruins, Hapsburg edifices and carved Venetian lions high on the façade of buildings of its west coast towns. For millennia, many cultures have flourished side by side. In this way, Istria's story is my family's story: my grandfather, Matteo, was born in Istria when it was Austria, lived in Istria when it was Italy, and left Istria when it was Yugoslavia. The town of his birth is now in Croatia.

In Istrian kitchens, Venetian seafood stews served with polenta sit side by side with hearty Hungarian-style goulash; ravioli with ricotta is effortlessly followed by Balkan flame-grilled meats on a skewer. All are accompanied by the salad greens and vegetables that grow in abundance on the peninsula, followed by desserts that you might find in a Viennese coffee shop, or in the cafes of Trieste.

Many dishes in this book are those of my childhood, of the vegetables and fruit that papà grew in his garden, what he or his *istriani* friends fished from Port Phillip Bay, the meats he bought from Alfredo the Italian butcher in Box Hill (the Melbourne suburb in which we first lived) – all of which mamma turned into the most delicious meals: stuffed artichokes, cabbage rolls, paper-thin crepes we called *palacinche*, eaten rolled up with home-made apricot or plum jam, and the best ricotta cake I have ever eaten. Other recipes have been inspired by cookbooks of the area, mostly written in Italian, and many from the time when Istria, Fiume and the nearby islands were part of the Hapsburg empire and Italy – ones I like to think my grandmother made for my grandfather as a young bride.

Further recipes have been drawn from my many recent visits to Istria, time spent with friends and family who live there, and generous meals in *konobe* (the Croatian word for restaurants). Times have changed substantially from my first visit to Istria in the 1970s, when the peninsula was under communist rule. The atmosphere of my father's home town (now Pula, Croatia), its market, and its people, is warm, inviting and abundant.

Food does not have borders. It speaks of the land and its people, of shared meals and cultures, of the past and the present, of family and community.

A NOTE ON NAMES & SPELLINGS

I refer to the names of towns in Istria and the surrounds in Italian, in passages where to have it in two languages would interfere with the flow of the writing. I grew up hearing the names of these places in Italian, often in our dialect, and it is the way I still speak of them. In recipes they are written in two languages: Italian, plus Croatian or Slovenian, depending on where the town is located. In Croatian and Slovenian, Istria is known as Istra.

HISTORICAL NOTES

Istria has been a country of many cultures living side by side for over a thousand years. For some 500 years, the western and southern parts of the Istrian peninsula were governed by the Republic of Venice, and the eastern part, which was referred to as Imperial Istria, by Austria.

With the rise of Napoleon and for most of the 1800s, the entire peninsula and its surrounds were part of the Austro–Hungarian empire, under the rule of the Hapsburgs.

After World War I, Istria – inclusive of Fiume/Rijeka, Zara/Zadar and many islands, the largest of which is Lussino/Lošinj – formed the Italian region of Venezia Giulia. After World War II, these areas were assigned to Yugoslavia, until its collapse in the early 1990s.

Istria is now split between Croatia and Slovenia, with a narrow northern strip around the fishing village of Muggia, which is part of Italy. After Croatians and Slovenes, Italians are the most populous ethnic group of Istria.

Soups

Zuppe

A nourishing soup was always welcome in my *nonna* (grandmother) Stefania's home in via Petilia in Pola/Pula. My father Nello and his sister Nives would come home from school just after one o'clock, ravenous, and find a bowl of steaming *minestra* or *zuppa* (soup) waiting for them on the kitchen table. I have been told my *nonna* would make a soup for her children every day; in winter a heavier soup, with beans, lentils or corn, and in summer with zucchini (courgettes) or tomatoes, reflecting the seasons and what was growing in the garden.

This soup is based on Caterina Prato's *zuppa di lenticchie* (lentil soup). I have added black barley to my version, as it is one of my favourite grains. It is cooked separately and stirred in at the end, soaking up much of the excess liquid. A dash of vinegar, as suggested by Caterina, is added just before serving. It balances the dish beautifully, lending an unexpected depth to what is otherwise a rather simple *zuppa*. If you cannot find black barley, use pearl barley and reduce the cooking time, as black barley takes a bit longer to cook.

Lentil & barley soup
(Zuppa di orzo e lenticchie)

Serves 4

200 g (7 oz) black barley
2 tablespoons extra virgin
  olive oil
15 g (½ oz) unsalted butter
1 brown onion, finely diced
1 garlic clove, chopped
200 g (7 oz) puy lentils or tiny
  blue-green lentils, washed
1 rosemary stalk
1.5 litres (51 fl oz) boiling water
sea salt and freshly cracked
  black pepper
3 tablespoons red wine vinegar,
  plus extra to serve

Bring a pot of salted water to the boil, add the barley and leave to cook at a rapid simmer. Taste the barley periodically and check how firm it is; it should be almost cooked through after 40 minutes. Once cooked to your liking, drain the barley and set aside.

While the barley is cooking, start the soup base by warming the olive oil and butter in a large heavy-based pan over medium–low heat. Add the onion and sauté for 15 minutes or so, until translucent but not yet starting to brown, stirring occasionally. Add the garlic and cook until fragrant.

Add the lentils, rosemary and boiling water, then cover and cook for about 25 minutes, or until the lentils start to soften, but still retain their shape. Skim off the impurities that rise to the surface and stir every now and then, adding salt and pepper to taste.

Add the cooked barley and cook for another 5 minutes or so, until the soup has thickened. Remove the rosemary sprig. Add the vinegar, salt to taste, and plenty of black pepper.

Serve warm or at room temperature, with extra red wine vinegar to the side. Fresh crusty bread is a good accompaniment to this soup and makes it a complete meal, and is how I like to think my *nonna* Stefania would have served it.

In late winter, my father planted borlotti (cranberry) beans in the garden. On the cusp of summer, some would be podded and eaten fresh, often in a salad; a few were set aside to be planted the following season; and the rest were dried and stored for cooking through the year. The dried ones usually ended up in a hearty wintery soup called *iota*. My father loved *iota*. It was a dish of memories of Istria for him, and Mamma would make it often, using the recipe below. It is not a pretty soup, but so delicious – thick with beans and flavoured with a ham hock, cured pork sausage (*luganiga de cragno*), or the left-over bone from a leg of prosciutto. At the end of cooking, a good quantity of sauerkraut is stirred in, adding welcome acidity to this rather rich, dense dish. The depth of flavour more than makes up for its rather beige appearance.

If using dried beans, you will need to soak them overnight; you could use tinned beans to save time. Both kidney beans and borlotti beans work well in this soup – I often use a combination of the two. If you have trouble finding cured pork sausage, use chorizo in its place.

Livia's bean & sauerkraut soup

(Iota)

Serves 4–6

400 g (2 cups) dried borlotti
   (cranberry) beans and/or red
   kidney beans
1 large potato, peeled and
   roughly chopped
1 small carrot, roughly chopped
2 fresh bay leaves
2 cured pork sausages, cut
   into chunks
100 g (3½ oz) pancetta, finely
   diced
1 tablespoon extra virgin
   olive oil, plus extra if needed
1 large brown onion, finely
   chopped
2 garlic cloves, finely chopped
400 g (14 oz) sauerkraut
sea salt and freshly cracked
   black pepper

Place the beans in a bowl, cover with plenty of water and allow to soak for 8 hours, or overnight.

Drain the beans and place in a large heavy-based lidded saucepan, together with the potato, carrot and bay leaves. Add 1.5 litres (51 fl oz) of water, cover and bring to the boil, then reduce the heat to medium. Skim off any impurities that float to the surface. After about 15 minutes, add the sausage chunks. Simmer for a further 15–25 minutes, until the beans are cooked through, but still maintaining their shape, and the potato and carrot are tender. (Note that borlotti beans take a bit longer to cook than kidney beans if using a combination.)

While the beans are cooking, place the pancetta in a frying pan with the olive oil and cook over medium–low heat for about 10 minutes, until it softens and releases its fat (do not let it brown). Add the onion (and a splash more oil if needed) and cook for another 10–15 minutes, until the onion is soft and translucent. Add the garlic and cook for a few more minutes, until fragrant. Turn off the heat and set aside.

Once the beans are cooked, scoop out half the beans with a slotted spoon, as well as the sausage chunks and bay leaves. Purée the rest of the soup using a hand-held blender, then return the beans and sausage to the pan, along with the sautéed pancetta mixture, setting the heat to low.

Drain the sauerkraut, then add it to the soup; if you like the sour taste, you may like to add some of the sour liquid from the sauerkraut. Stir well and warm on the stove for about 5 minutes. Add salt and pepper to taste and serve warm (not hot).

Iota is even nicer the next day or the one after that, though you may need to add a little water before reheating, as it tends to thicken as it cools.

When the summer sun shines, tomatoes are at their sweetest, ripening on the vine and bursting with flavour. There is nothing as flavoursome as fat, round, ripe, in-season tomatoes, which are what I use to make this soup. Pale and tasteless winter tomatoes grown in a hothouse will be a pale comparison to summer beauties. Cream is added to the soup right at the end, which cools it to just the right temperature to enjoy on a warm summer evening. You could serve it with a crisp green salad and call it supper. It is simple and takes less than 30 minutes to make.

I use a hand-cranked food mill – *passatutto* – to crush both the cooked potatoes and tomatoes, and sift out the skin and seeds. The *passatutto* (which literally means 'sieve everything') is a wonderful addition to a kitchen; it is inexpensive, and imagine all the time you will save from not having to peel vegetables for soup. If you do not have a food mill, use a potato masher to mash the vegetables in the pot, then pass through a sieve to remove the seeds and skin.

Summer tomato soup
(Minestra di pomodori)

Serves 4–6

1 litre (4 cups) Really good vegetable stock (page244) – or use a good-quality vegetable stock (bouillon) cube
60 ml (¼ cup) extra virgin olive oil, plus an extra splash
1 large garlic clove, peeled
1 kg (2 lb 3 oz) large, ripe in-season tomatoes
500 g (1 lb 2 oz) old or floury potatoes (the ones that are good for gnocchi), washed well
sea salt and freshly cracked black pepper
a few slices of sourdough or other crusty bread, preferably a few days old
150 ml (5 fl oz) pouring (single/light) cream

Bring the stock to the boil.

Meanwhile, place the olive oil in a large heavy-based saucepan over medium heat. Finely chop the garlic, reserving one thick slice for later. Add the finely chopped garlic to the pan and sauté for a few minutes, until fragrant. Roughly chop the tomatoes and potatoes and add them to the pot. Allow them to warm through, then pour in the boiling stock. Add salt and pepper to taste, cover, then set the heat to low so that the vegetables can simmer.

While the soup is cooking, rub the reserved slice of garlic on the slices of bread. Cut into cubes and toss in olive oil. Place in a frying pan over medium–high heat and toast for a couple of minutes. Set aside.

Once the potato is cooked through (about 20 minutes), remove the pan from the heat. Pass the soup through a food mill, a few ladlefuls at a time, to strain out the skins and seeds. Return the soup to the pot, stir in the cream and season with salt and pepper to taste.

Serve warm or at room temperature. Scatter the toasted bread cubes over just before serving.

Eat the soup within a day or so. If you are planning to leave it for longer than this, leave the cream out, and add it just before you plan to serve.

This is a light, soupy rice dish, delicious in its simplicity. It is based on a recipe by Iolanda de Vonderweid and makes the most of summer produce, using up the excess of zucchini and tomatoes from the garden in mid to late summer. I like to add parmesan rinds to the soup, like my mother did. When you are nearing the end of your block of parmesan, and it becomes harder to grate, scrape off any paint or wax that is on the outer side, then cut it into bite-sized chunks and drop it into soups or risotto for a good part of the cooking process. You can also freeze the cleaned and chopped rinds. It is a brilliant addition to your dish, and makes you a good home economist. There might even be fights over those delicious pieces of softened rind when the soup is ladled into bowls.

Zucchini & rice soup
(Minestra di zucchini e riso)

Serves 4

300 g (10½ oz) ripe in-season tomatoes (or a bit over half a tin of good-quality peeled tomatoes)
1 small onion, finely diced
2–3 tablespoons extra virgin olive oil, plus extra for drizzling
4 anchovies (omit for a vegetarian version)
750 g (1 lb 11½ oz) zucchini (courgettes)
1 litre (4 cups) Really good vegetable stock (page 244) – or use a good-quality vegetable stock (bouillon) cube
2 basil stalks, plus extra basil leaves to serve
parmesan rinds (optional)
175 g (6½ oz) short-grain or medium-grain rice
sea salt and freshly cracked black pepper
grated parmesan, to serve

Bring a small saucepan of water to the boil. Using a sharp knife, cut a cross into the base of the tomatoes and plunge them into the boiling water. Scoop them out with a slotted spoon when they come to the boil. Peel off the tomato skins and cut into quarters (or eighths, depending on their size). Remove the seeds and cut into chunks. (If using tinned tomatoes, chop them in half, then carefully remove the seeds with a spoon.) Set aside.

Place the onion, olive oil and anchovies in a large heavy-based saucepan over medium–low heat. Cook for about 10 minutes, or until the onion has softened.

Chop the zucchini into 1 cm (½ in) rounds and cut each round into quarters. Add the zucchini and tomato to the pan and stir until they warm through.

Meanwhile, in a separate saucepan, heat the stock until it is boiling, then add to the vegetables. Drop in the basil stalks and parmesan rinds (if using) and simmer, covered, for 5 minutes. Next, drop in the rice. Cover and simmer for another 10 minutes, or until the rice is almost cooked through.

Turn off the heat and allow to sit, covered, for 5–10 minutes, until the rice has cooked through completely. A lot of the stock will have been absorbed.

Taste for salt and add freshly cracked black pepper if you like. Serve warm or at room temperature, with grated parmesan, a drizzle of olive oil and a few basil leaves to garnish.

THAT SUMMER
SHE BECAME
MY BEST FRIEND

My *zio* (uncle) Mario loved sailing. He had a boat called *Mony*, moored in Monfalcone, near Trieste. Every summer he and his wife, Clara, would sail *Mony* down the coast of Istria to his home town of Pola. There they would meet their friends, arriving from all over Italy to spend the summer camping by the beach at Stoia.

One summer, when I was 15, I joined them. I watched on as the women selected the spot that would be best for the communal tent, and the men worked to assemble it, striped sheets of canvas flapping in the breeze as they cleared away pine needles and broken branches. My aunt Clara had told me that their friends Gianna and Bobo, who lived in Pola, would join us on weekends, and they had a daughter who was my age. Her name was Ksenija.

Ksenija became my best friend that summer. We rowed on a rubber dinghy at Stoia, tanned lying on the deck of *Mony*, talked about boys in our shared dialect, walked along the streets of Pola, stopping to admire the Roman arena and the forum, hung out at the apartment where she lived, ate home-cooked meals prepared by Gianna and her grandmother Vera, traipsed through the pine forest and laughed the way teenagers laugh, with the sheer joy of summer and holidays.

Ksenija's father had a beautiful yellow-and-black wooden sailing boat called *Grga*. The north-eastern Adriatic has some of the cleanest waters in the world, and fish are plentiful. We sailed the *Grga* down to the remote island of Unie south of Pola, with *Mony* cruising alongside. The waters were turquoise and clear; you could see the tails and fins of the huge silvery fish in the water many metres below. We dropped nets to catch our dinner and later feasted on grilled fish with lemon, salads, bread and fruit. We dropped anchor for the night, and the next day pulled into the tiny port of the island; the warm air smelt of salt, rosemary and pine as Ksenija and I walked arm in arm along the promenade.

It was some 20 years later when I next saw Ksenija. And I have seen her many times since. Nothing has changed; although she is not family, she feels like family. She and her husband, Tomi, take us to restaurants, sightseeing and to visit her mother, Gianna, who greets us with home-made cake. We all sit on the back terrace, looking out to the giant walnut tree, sipping stovetop coffee with nips of grappa. Gianna tells stories of my family and the times she has spent with them. I am immersed in memories of that summer by the beach, the hot sun on my back, the rhythm of the waves, Ksenija and I laughing at my uncle Mario's jokes and the shared meals of mussels, bream, tomatoes, olive oil and bread. It feels like home.

*Quell'estate divenne la mia
amica del cuore*

On a trip to Istria some years ago, long-time family friend Gianna gave me a recipe for her fennel soup, which I wrote on a piece of paper. Back home in Australia, I searched high and low for the recipe. I knew it had fennel, potatoes and garlic, and maybe fennel fronds, but could not remember what else. I did not want to bother Gianna again, confessing how careless I had been with her recipe. So I made my own version with roasted fennel bulbs, which really brings out their aniseed-like taste, which I adore.

While writing the final draft of this book, and after a big spring-clean, I found the recipe, deep in a side pocket, among train ticket stubs and postcards. Reading it, I realised it is quite different from the one I had made, with a large bunch of fennel fronds front and centre of the dish; there were also borlotti (cranberry) beans and farro. I decided to keep the recipe I had made, as I thought about Gianna quite a lot while I was in the kitchen making the soup – the lovely terrace with the cloth-covered table that looks into the garden, and the chats we would have over stovetop coffee. So Gianna, this soup might not be yours, but it was made for you.

Roasted fennel soup
(Vellutata di finocchio arrosto)

Serves 6

2 large fennel bulbs, about 1 kg
  (2 lb 3 oz)
2 medium potatoes, about 500 g
  (1 lb 2 oz)
1 large onion
4 garlic cloves
60 ml (¼ cup) extra virgin olive
  oil, plus extra if needed
2 teaspoons dried oregano
sea salt and freshly cracked
  black pepper
1.5 litres (51 fl oz) Really good
  vegetable stock (page 244) –
  or use a good-quality vegetable
  stock (bouillon) cube
crusty bread, to serve

Preheat the oven to 200°C (400°F) fan-forced.

Start by preparing the vegetables. Trim the fronds and stalks off the fennel and cut the bulbs into wedges. (You can include some of the stalks, but not if they are too green and spindly, as they will burn in the oven.) Reserve some of the fennel fronds for garnishing. Peel and chop each potato into about eight pieces. Peel the onion and cut into wedges. Remove the outer skin of the garlic, leaving a few layers intact, and smash the cloves with the side of knife.

Divide the vegetables between two baking trays, drizzling them with the olive oil. Scatter 1 teaspoon of the oregano and some salt over each tray. Toss the vegetables with your hands so they are well coated with olive oil. If it seems like there isn't enough olive oil, add a bit more.

Roast for 15–25 minutes, until the vegetables are cooked through; the cooking time really depends on the size you have cut them. They should be fork-tender and starting to turn golden. Check the vegetables after 10 minutes to make sure they are not burning. If they are scorching, remove the trays from the oven and carefully re-toss the vegetables (using a spoon or tongs, as they will be quite hot).

While the vegetables are roasting, place the vegetable stock in a large saucepan (large enough to hold all the vegetables) and bring to the boil.

Carefully drop the roasted vegetables into the stock and squeeze the garlic cloves into the soup. Bring back to the boil and after a few minutes, remove the pan from the heat.

Using a hand-held blender, purée the vegetables until a thick creamy soup forms. Place the pan back on the stove, and add extra stock or water as needed to reach your preferred consistency. Bring back to the boil, then simmer for a few more minutes. Add salt and freshly cracked black pepper to taste.

Serve bowls of hot soup garnished with a few reserved fennel fronds and crusty bread on the side.

Appetisers

Antipasti

Salty sea air, waves lapping the rocky shore and a never-ending chorus of seagulls provided the backdrop of my first summer in Pola/Pula in the early 1970s. I remember exploring sea caves on a tiny boat, paddling in the bluest of waters with my father, and working up a huge appetite. I was only six, but the memory is strong: platters of tomatoes, halved and topped with a tasty garlicky crumb sitting beside fried sardines that we ate by the beach near Stoia/Stoja.

You will need fat, sweet-tasting tomatoes to make this dish – a favourite of mine since that summer. They should be firm but ripe, and it is better if they are all the same size, around 250 g (9 oz). How much filling you need depends on the size of the tomatoes. You can serve them as part of an antipasto platter, but they go really well with fish, especially oily fish like sardines and mackerel. Feel free to double the recipe, as they are equally lovely at room temperature the next day.

Baked tomatoes with parmesan, garlic & parsley
(Gratinata di pomodori)

Serves 4

5 large in-season tomatoes
sea salt and freshly cracked
  black pepper
45 g (1½ oz) dry breadcrumbs,
  preferably home-made
25 g (¼ cup) grated parmesan
2 garlic cloves, diced
handful of parsley leaves
extra virgin olive oil, for
  drizzling

Remove the stalks from four of the tomatoes. Cut the tomatoes in half horizontally, then scoop out the seeds and discard them, leaving the vertical walls in the middle of each tomato half intact. Reserve some of the liquid that is released from the tomatoes, as you may need a few teaspoons of this for the filling. Scatter salt on the tomato halves, then turn them upside down and place on a wire rack over a bowl so that the excess juice drains out. Let them sit that way for about 30 minutes. In the meantime, you can prepare the filling.

Preheat the oven to 170°C (340°F) fan-forced.

Cut the remaining tomato in half, scoop out the seeds and discard. Scoop the seedless tomato flesh from the shell and roughly chop. Place the tomato flesh in a mini food processor, together with the breadcrumbs, parmesan, garlic and parsley. Season with pepper and pulse. If the mixture is too dry to pulse, add some of the reserved tomato liquid; the filling should be fairly dry. Add salt to taste.

Spoon the filling into the eight tomato halves and place in a baking dish. Drizzle with olive oil and bake for 45–50 minutes. Check halfway and reduce the temperature if they are browning too quickly.

Serve warm or at room temperature. Store in an airtight container in the fridge and eat within a few days.

The Polesini family was the closest you got to Istrian nobility. The family owned lands within the castle of Montona/Motovun dating back to the 13th century; they built a Palladian-style villa and gardens (the Polesini Castle) near San Lorenzo/Sveti Lovreč, and in 1788 were given the title of Marquis by the Venetian Republic. They also owned the island of San Nicolò/Sveti Nicola, just off the coast of Paranzo/Poreč, which is where the Hungarian-born cookbook author, Margherita (Eta), lived with her husband, Marquis Gianpaolo Polesini.

Eta probably didn't need to write cookbooks to make a living, but she must have loved cooking and sharing her recipes. She wrote five paperback recipe books in the 1930s, largely inspired by the food of the Austro–Hungarian empire. The books were about entertaining guests, which would have been rather lovely in her castle on the family island in the Adriatic Sea. This recipe is inspired by one in her book on antipasti, which I managed to purchase from a vintage bookstore in Italy. The original recipe has ham in the *polpettine*, but I rather like making them vegetarian. They make a lovely addition to an antipasto platter. They are very moist, but you could serve them with a tiny dollop of mayonnaise to the side, as perhaps the Marchioness might have done.

Spinach 'meatballs'
(Polpettine di spinaci)

Makes 26–28

1 kg (2 lb 3 oz) English spinach
3 egg yolks
75 g (2¾ oz) unsalted butter,
    at room temperature
30 g (1 oz) parmesan, finely
    grated, plus extra to serve,
    if desired
zest of 1 lemon, plus extra to
    serve, if desired
100 g (1 cup) dry breadcrumbs
sea salt
extra virgin olive oil,
    for pan-frying
freshly cracked black pepper

Wash the spinach several times until it is clean of dirt or sand. Remove and discard the thick stalks and any damaged leaves. Place a large saucepan that will fit all the spinach over medium heat. Place the washed (and still wet) spinach in the pan and, using tongs, push it down until the heat starts wilting the spinach. This should only take a couple of minutes. When it has wilted completely, remove from the heat. Place in a colander to drain, then place the cooked leaves in a clean tea towel and squeeze all the excess water out. The spinach should be quite dry. Chop finely by hand or in a food processor, then set aside to cool.

Place the egg yolks in a large bowl and whisk briefly with a fork. Add the butter and mix it into the eggs with a spoon. Next, add the finely chopped spinach, mixing well, then the parmesan, lemon zest and about one-third of the breadcrumbs, and salt to taste. The mixture should be quite firm and you should be able to shape it into balls; add a few more breadcrumbs if needed.

Shape the mixture into walnut-shaped balls, about 20 g (¾ oz) in weight. Roll them in the remaining breadcrumbs. Heat a few tablespoons of olive oil in a large non-stick frying pan. Pan-fry the *polpettine* in batches, turning them over regularly for 5–6 minutes, or until they are golden all over.

Serve warm, topping with pepper and extra parmesan or lemon zest, if desired.

From an antique bookseller in Italy, I purchased three of the five paperback cookbooks written by Marchesa Eta Polesini in the 1930s. The books all have the same title: *Cosa prepare per i miei ospiti* ('What I prepare for my guests'), each with a different subtitle, including 'Fish and meat' and 'Soups, leafy greens and legumes'. One of the Marchesa's recipes is *Bretzel alle nocciole,* savoury hazelnut and cheese biscuits that are shaped like a pretzel. They seemed a bit fiddly to make into twisted shapes, but they also make lovely round biscotti. Although she served these to her guests with tea, they are even better with a glass of Malvasia wine, or as part of an *aperitivo* platter with cured meats, pickled cucumbers and cheese.

Hazelnut cheese biscuits
(Biscotti salati alle nocciole)

Makes about 30

200 g (1⅓ cups) plain
    (all-purpose) flour
50 g (⅓ cup) spelt flour
    (or wholemeal/whole
    wheat flour)
80 g (2¾ oz) hazelnuts, ground
    to a flour
¼ teaspoon sea salt
¼ teaspoon ground nutmeg
big pinch of cayenne pepper
60 g (2 oz) emmental or
    jarlsberg, finely grated
90 g (3 oz) unsalted butter,
    softened
1 egg, lightly beaten
1–2 tablespoons milk,
    for brushing
¼ teaspoon sea salt flakes

Place the flours, hazelnut flour, salt and spices in a large bowl. Whisk briefly to combine. Add the cheese, butter and egg. Mix with a large spoon and then with your hands, to mix and bring the dough together, adding a few teaspoons of water. Taste and check there is enough salt.

Shape into two logs, each about 12 cm (4¾ in) in length. Wrap tightly in baking paper, twisting the ends so that the dough parcel is sealed off. Rest in the fridge for about an hour, or even overnight.

Preheat the oven to 160°C (320°F) fan-forced. Line two baking trays with baking paper. These biscuits do not spread, so you can place them quite close to each other.

Unwrap the dough logs, then slice each log into rounds, about 5–6 mm (¼ in) thick. I used a 6 cm (2½ in) cookie cutter to help me make the perfect round, bashing the surface with the side of a wide knife to make the top flat. Brush with a little milk. Crush a few salt flakes with your fingertips and scatter them over each biscuit before placing in the oven.

Bake for about 14 minutes, or until the biscuits turn golden around the edges. Cool on a wire rack. Store in an airtight container for 4–5 days.

When I was in primary school, we lived in the Melbourne suburb of Box Hill, in a house my father had built in the early 1950s. Mamma's brothers lived in adjoining self-built houses, and we could slip into each other's backyards through openings in the back fence. It was easy dropping in and there was always something delicious being prepared in the kitchen, from fried sardines and meat *polpette* to sweet *crostoli* and ricotta cake. Crumbed and fried eggplant (aubergine), which we called *melanzane apanade*, was one of my favourites. In the early evening, with the summer sun still perched in the sky, the aroma would call us from over the fence. We would run through the vegetable garden, through the doorway in the fence and climb the back steps into the kitchen, as if in a trance. Just-fried slices of eggplant would be laid out on a bed of paper napkins to collect the excess oil, and my aunt Dina would have scattered on some salt. We would pick up a slice, holding it with a paper napkin, and squeeze on some fresh lemon juice before biting into it.

Crumbed eggplant
(Melanzane apanade)

Serves 6

1 large eggplant (aubergine),
    about 500 g (1 lb 2 oz)
75 g (½ cup) plain (all-purpose)
    flour
115 g (1 generous cup) dry
    breadcrumbs, preferably
    homemade
2 eggs
250 ml (1 cup) milk
sea salt
olive oil, for pan-frying
lemon wedges, to serve

Wash the eggplant and pat dry. Cut into even slices, about 7–8 mm (⅓ in) thick.

Prepare two plates and a wide bowl – place the flour on one plate, the breadcrumbs on the other plate, and lightly whisk the eggs and milk in the bowl with a good pinch of salt.

Dip one slice of eggplant at a time first in the flour, making sure the slice is evenly coated; then in the egg wash (you may like to use forks to help you); then finally in the breadcrumbs. If you would like to make a double-crumbed layer, put the crumbed eggplant slice back in the egg wash and then again in the breadcrumbs. If you double-crumb you will need more egg wash and breadcrumbs.

Place a good glug of olive oil in a wide frying pan. It should cover the surface of the pan completely by about 3–4 mm (⅙–¼ in). Place over medium heat for a few minutes, or until it warms up.

Fry the eggplant slices in batches, turning over after about 4 minutes. The crumb should be golden but not too dark (if it is, reduce the heat a little). The other side should take 2–3 minutes to cook through. Remove with tongs and place on paper towel to absorb the excess oil. Repeat until you have used up all the eggplant. If you notice that the pan is dry, or has lots of breadcrumbs in it, remove from the heat, wipe the pan clean, add a bit more oil and continue frying.

Enjoy warm or at room temperature, with plenty of sea salt flakes and a good squeeze of lemon juice.

I WILL DROP EVERYONE
AND EVERYTHING AND
TRAVEL THE WORLD

My father completed military training in 1939 and 1940, the early years of World War II. Military training was compulsory, and after some time training at a sports academy in Rome, he went to Tuscany to complete his officer training. He loved the physicality of those years, and the mateship with men who became lifelong friends. This was, of course, before he went to the front, when things became substantially different and more difficult.

He was not a great letter writer, but kept up a correspondence with his first cousin Alide, from 1940 through to 1945. I found the letters a couple of years ago when we were packing up the family home so it could be sold. The bundle was at the back of a cupboard, wrapped up with a ribbon. It contained letters from my father to his cousin, as well as war-time postcards written by my grandfather Matteo, in his small, precise Austrian handwriting, to his sister Luigia, Alide's mother. We had no idea these letters existed until then.

I painstakingly deciphered and translated the letters, and it was through this trail of correspondence that we were able to map his travels during those war years – from Arezzo in Tuscany, to Athens in Greece, and then to Dolen Ciflik, a prisoner of war camp in Varna on the shores of the Black Sea in Romania. These were times he rarely talked about.

The letters are initially playful, describing the life of an officer in training. Once in Greece he writes of excursions to Attica, Marathon and Salamini, places he had only known through history books, and of happy times that the cousins had spent together, harvesting grapes at their grandparents' property in Chersano in central Istria. They give insight into his hopes and dreams: 'When this has ended, I will drop everyone and everything and travel the world.'

Later letters take on a more sombre tone, where he writes, 'I hope it (the war) ends soon, and well.' For him, the war ending well meant he would return home to his beloved Pola, and that it would remain part of Italy. After the war he did return. A photo taken in front of the town hall in one of the main squares of Pola in July 1946 shows him, and all the other council workers, smiling in the sun of what was to be, for many, their last summer in Istria. In 1947, as new European borders were drawn, most of the former region of Venezia Giulia – parts of Istria, Fiume and dozens of small islands off the coast – were ceded to communist Yugoslavia. He and his family, together with a large proportion of the Istrian–Italian population, left Istria by ship, with as many of their belongings as they could carry, sailing to Trieste.

From these difficult times, however, there were positives. In mid 1947, in the town of Monfalcone, he met sunny-natured Livia. And in 1950, my parents migrated to Australia by ship. It was then that my father was able to fulfil one of his dreams: to travel the world.

Pianto tutti e tutto e vado
via per il mondo

Trieste, like Pola/Pula, was part of Austria in the 1800s, and many food traditions from that period remain, in restaurants, delicatessens and on family tables. My father spent some time in Trieste during his military training, as he would pass through there on the way to Pola from Rome or Arezzo, often stopping to see friends. *Liptauer* is one of the dishes he enjoyed, a creamy spicy dip traditionally made with soft sheep's milk cheese, flavoured with paprika and cumin and eaten spread on dark bread.

Soft sheep's milk cheese is not widely available, but you can make a good approximation of the taste of traditional *liptauer* at home using ricotta, mascarpone and sour cream. I like to top the spread with capers, which gives it an extra savoury hit. Alternative toppings you might like to experiment with include finely sliced spring onion (scallion), a thin sliver of anchovy fillet or, for a summer version, a sprinkling of finely diced tomato and plums.

Ricotta spread with paprika
(Crema stile liptauer)

Serves 6–8

a few teaspoons salted capers
150 g (5½ oz) ricotta, well
  drained
50 g (1¾ oz) cream cheese
30 g (1 oz) sour cream
1 teaspoon sweet paprika
1 teaspoon French mustard
½ teaspoon caraway seeds,
  crushed
¼ teaspoon cumin seeds,
  crushed
splash of white wine (optional)
rye bread, thinly sliced

Soak the capers in a small bowl of water for about 10 minutes while you prepare the dip, to remove the excess salt. Drain and set aside, ready to use.

Place the ricotta, cream cheese and sour cream in a mini food processor and blend until smooth. Add the paprika, mustard, caraway and cumin seeds, either stirring by hand or using the processor. If the mixture is too thick (it should be like a dip), add a splash of wine (if using). The taste is quite personal, so add more mustard, paprika, cumin or caraway if this is to your liking.

Spread the dip on thin slices of fresh or lightly toasted rye bread, topped with a few capers or an alternative topping. Serve immediately.

Store the spread in an airtight container in the fridge for a few days.

Cookbook author Mady Fast attributes the recipe of *polenta co' le broze* (crusty polenta) to Mariuccia Giovannini from Isola/Izola. It is the simplest of dishes, with wedges of firm polenta, olive oil and anchovy fillets, but very tasty as an *aperitivo* with a glass of chilled wine or a beer to soak up the deliciously salty flavours. Although I am not a fan of instant polenta, it works well in this dish, as you can whip it up with little effort when guests drop by unexpectedly in the late afternoon.

Polenta wedges with anchovy oil
(Polenta co' le broze)

Serves 4–6

sea salt
125 g (4½ oz) instant polenta
2 tablespoons olive oil
4 oil-preserved anchovy fillets, chopped

Before starting, prepare two baking trays that are at least 20 cm x 30 cm (8 in x 12 in) in size, by dampening the bases with water. Set aside until needed.

Bring 500 ml (2 cups) water to the boil, season with salt and pour in the polenta in a slow, steady stream, whisking the whole time. Once you have added all the polenta, swap the whisk for a wooden spoon, and stir continuously for about 3 minutes, or until the polenta becomes very thick and difficult to stir.

Tip the polenta onto one of the trays, flattening the polenta using the wet side of the other tray, and shaping it into a rectangle. (The damp surface helps to prevent the polenta sticking.) Allow to cool for at least 10 minutes, then cut into logs, about the width of two fingers (you should have 16–18).

Place the oil and anchovy in a small saucepan over low heat. Cook for a few minutes, or until the anchovy starts to dissolve. Set aside.

Heat a chargrill pan over medium–high heat, then cook the polenta logs for several minutes so that charred black lines form. Using tongs, turn them over and brush the surface of each log with the anchovy-infused oil while the undersides finish cooking.

Serve immediately and enjoy while warm.

My father loved seafood, especially sardines. Growing up in Pola/Pula, right by the beach, family meals were more often than not bream, mackerel or sardines, and in Australia, when he did the weekly grocery shopping on a Friday afternoon, my father would often buy fish. I would watch him gutting and filleting the fish at the sink. With sardines, he would fold the fish at the head, then use his finger to make a slit along its length and remove the head, entrails and spine in one deft move. He taught me his nifty and very quick method for cleaning sardines but, I must admit, I find it is a lot easier buying them already filleted.

This was one of his favourite dishes. A mix of garlic and parsley is sandwiched between two fillets of sardines, which my mother would carefully then roll in breadcrumbs and pop under the grill (broiler). I love to make the same stuffing, then coat the sardines in flour, egg wash and breadcrumbs and pan-fry them, before serving with a good squeeze of lemon juice. If you enjoy oily fish like sardines, you will love this dish.

Stuffed sardines
(Sardele ripiene)

Serves 4–8

16 large sardines, filleted
3–4 tablespoons parsley leaves,
    finely chopped
1 large garlic clove, finely
    chopped
plain (all-purpose) flour,
    for coating
50 g (½ cup) dry breadcrumbs
1 egg
a splash of milk
sea salt
extra virgin olive oil,
    for pan-frying
sea salt flakes, to serve
lemon wedges, to serve

Wash the sardine fillets and pat dry. Lay eight sardine fillets, skin side down, on a work surface (I use a chopping board that I devote solely to fish). Scatter some parsley and garlic down the centre of each fillet. Cover each with a sardine fillet and pat down.

Prepare two plates and a shallow bowl – place the flour on one plate, the breadcrumbs on the other, and lightly whisk the egg and milk in the bowl with a good pinch of salt.

Carefully place one of the sardine parcels in the flour, then carefully turn it over to flour the other side. Next, dunk it gently in the egg mixture, turning it over with the help of a fork. Finally, coat the fillet in the breadcrumbs. You will need to be careful when crumbing the sardines so that the filling does not fall out. Repeat.

Place a good glug of olive oil in a wide frying pan. It should cover the surface of the pan completely by about 3–4 mm (⅙–¼ in). Place over medium heat for a few minutes, or until the oil warms up.

Fry the sardines in batches, turning over after about 4 minutes. The crumb should be golden but not too dark (if it is, reduce the heat a bit). The other side should take 2–3 minutes to cook through. Remove with tongs and place on paper towel to absorb the excess oil. Repeat until finished. If you notice that the pan is dry, or has lots of breadcrumbs in it, remove from the heat, wipe the pan clean, add a bit more oil and continue frying.

Enjoy the sardines warm or at room temperature, with plenty of sea salt flakes and a good squeeze of lemon juice.

We call asparagus *sparisi*. In Istria, spindly asparagus grows wild and is sold from buckets on the roadside. I always buy my asparagus spears loose – big handfuls of them – and store them in the fridge with their stems in a glass of water, much like a bunch of flowers. They last for ages that way.

The quantity of asparagus in the recipe below depends on the size of the spears. I use the thinnest ones I can find, so each prosciutto-wrapped bundle has three or four thin spears. If you can only find medium to thick spears, modify the quantities accordingly. Similarly, with the prosciutto, if the slices are large, feel free to cut them in half lengthways.

Asparagus prosciutto wraps
(Asparagi con il prosciutto)

Serves 4

36 thin asparagus spears
  (or 24 medium ones)
sea salt and freshly cracked
  black pepper
iced water
6–12 slices prosciutto,
  thinly sliced
2 tablespoons extra virgin
  olive oil, plus extra to serve
1 handful of parsley leaves,
  finely chopped, plus extra
  to serve
1 garlic clove, finely chopped
zest of 1 lemon
55 g (2 oz) parmesan,
  thinly shaved

Preheat the oven to 200°C (400°F) fan-forced. Line a shallow baking tray that will fit all the asparagus in a single layer.

Trim the woody ends from the asparagus and make sure the spears are approximately the same length. Bring a large saucepan of salted water to the boil and drop in the asparagus spears. Cook them for a few minutes, depending on how thick they are; I cook thin spears for 2 minutes. You need to partially cook the asparagus, so it still has a bit of bite. Plunge the spears into iced water, then drain, pat dry and set aside.

If you have large or wide slices of prosciutto, cut them in half lengthways.

Place the olive oil, parsley, garlic and lemon zest in a shallow tray. Season with salt and pepper. Drag the asparagus spears through the oil so they are well coated.

Depending on the size of the spears, wrap one, two or three spears in a slice of prosciutto, on an angle if needed, so that most of the spears, except for the two ends, are covered in prosciutto. Lay them on the prepared tray and repeat until you have a single layer of asparagus bundles. Scatter the parmesan over the top.

Bake on the top shelf of the oven for about 12 minutes, until the cheese has melted and the prosciutto is crispy. Garnish with extra parsley and drizzle on a bit of olive oil if you like. Allow to cool for a few minutes before serving.

SHE SHED MANY TEARS FOR THE LOSS OF HER HOME TOWN

I call her *santola* Gemma; she is my godmother. She was in the same class at school as my uncle Mario, our friend Bibo and my aunt Nives in Pola. I love chatting to her on the phone and listening to the stories she tells of the old days. She has an incredible memory for a 95-year-old.

She recalls that the war years were very hard. Pola was a naval base, and a target for bombings. There were food shortages, so the working head of the family would, where possible, send his family to stay with friends in the country, where it was safer and easier to feed everyone – all you needed was land to grow vegetables and a small yard to keep chickens. The men stayed behind, Gemma's father, Angelo, and my grandfather, Matteo, working side by side at the post office, cheering each other up and looking out for each other. Once the bombing stopped, they called their families back home. The train line had been cut and travel by boat was no longer safe – so Gemma, her mother and brothers and sister walked some 50 kilometres (30 miles) from Rovigno back to Pola and to the arms of Angelo.

Back in war-time Pola, Gemma remembers always being hungry. Her family lived in council flats, on the third floor, and they relied on food vouchers. Each family member had a voucher for their 100 g (3½ oz) or so daily bread allowance. In the mornings, Gemma would walk to the bakery with the family's vouchers to get the bread for eight. She would eat her portion as she walked along the road home, careful to not eat too much lest she dip into the rations for the others in her family.

As hard as it was living through those war years, there were benefits of living on the third floor with a balcony. Gemma laughs as she tells a story of her future husband Mario. Unbeknownst to her, he would stand on the street corner and look up to the third floor, admiring the dark-haired beauty from afar. He did not tell her until after they started dating, which she says was lucky – if she had seen him staring up at her back then, she may not have married him!

After the war, the newlyweds felt the need to distance themselves from war-ravaged Europe, hoping for a future with possibilities. Gemma and Mario were the first of our Istrian friends to migrate to Australia. They arrived in December 1949, and were immediately shuttled by train to Bonegilla migrant camp, some three hours from Melbourne. It looked and felt like the middle of nowhere. Gemma remembers her first Christmas in Australia, at the camp. Christmas music was playing, she was clutching her expectant belly, and shedding tears for the loss of her home town of Pola.

They settled into life in Melbourne and purchased land by the bay, a place that would remind them of home. My father, Nello, came across his former school friend quite by chance, through another Italian friend. Gemma tells me of the first time he came to visit them in their newly built bungalow. They had very little money, but were making do and welcoming their *istriani* friends with open arms. Gemma made him a coffee on the stovetop, excusing the lack of *cuciarini* (teaspoons) to stir the sugar. *'Non te preoccupar Gemma, te li porto mi'* ('Don't worry Gemma, I will get you some'), my father replied.

Next time he dropped in at the bungalow, Nello was carrying a bunch of forks, spoons and knives. They appeared to be a set, as they all had the same word on the handle: COFA. Gemma and Mario thanked him, but couldn't help wondering where they came from. Nello was somewhat evasive, saying they had somehow fallen into his hands, but they were a gift for their new home in Australia. I laughed so much when I heard this. COFA stood for 'Commonwealth of Australia' – government-issue cutlery from the Williamstown migrant camp.

*Gho pianto tanto
pensando de Pola*

My godfather, who I called *santolo* Mario was one of my father's closest friends from Pola/Pula. I chat to his widow, Gemma, often, and we talk about the old days and how Mario loved to cook for the groups of *istriani* who would drop over for a game of cards. This was one of his favourite and most popular dishes – mussels baked in the oven with a crispy and delicious savoury topping of anchovy fillets, garlic and parmesan.

Mario's baked mussels
(Mussoli al forno)

Makes 24

24 live mussels, about 1 kg
  (2 lb 3 oz)
1 small ripe tomato
10 g (¼ oz) oil-preserved
  anchovy fillets, finely chopped
2 tablespoons parsley leaves,
  finely chopped
1 garlic clove, finely chopped
  or crushed
2 tablespoons extra virgin
  olive oil
50 g (½ cup) dry breadcrumbs
25 g (¼ cup) grated parmesan

Scrub, debeard and wash the mussels in plenty of cold water.

Place a large lidded frying pan over high heat and add the mussels. Cover and allow them to sit there for a minute, shaking the pan once or twice, then lift the lid to check if any have opened. Using tongs, remove the ones that have steamed open, then put the lid back on. Give the pan an occasional shake, then check again, removing the opened mussels. Do this for up to 5 minutes. If any remain closed, discard them.

Discard one half-shell from each mussel and inspect the contents. Trim any beards that remain, and gently prise the mussel from the shell if it is attached. Place all the opened mussels, in their half shell, on a lined baking tray.

Preheat the oven to 180°C (350°F) fan-forced.

To make the topping, finely chop the tomato, separating the seeds from the flesh, and reserving the liquid. Place the tomato, anchovy, parsley, garlic, olive oil, breadcrumbs and parmesan in a bowl and stir with a spoon to form a thick crumbly paste. Add some of the reserved juice from the tomato – a few teaspoons should do – to bring the crumbs together. Spoon teaspoons of the mixture on top of the mussels.

Bake for 12–15 minutes, or until the topping is golden. Let the mussels cool for a few minutes before serving.

The mussels should be eaten directly off the shell, though some prefer to use a fork.

Pasta, gnocchi & risotto

Pasta, gnocchi e risotto

There is nothing as lovely as home-made pasta. Dried shop-bought pasta has a totally different texture from what you make at home in your own kitchen. *Macaruni* is the Istrian version of *pici* from central Italy, though much shorter, made with just flour, water and a pinch of salt. They are dense, chewy and require no special equipment to make – just a bit of elbow grease, and fast-moving hands. Small balls of dough are placed between the palms of your hands, which are rubbed together vigorously, shaping the dough into an elongated shape that is fatter in the middle and tapered at the ends.

I ate this shape of pasta in a restaurant near Valle/Bale dining with my friend Ksenija, though she called them *pljukanci* (pl-ee-oo-kan-si), which is not remotely like the word I knew them by. I sought advice from a Facebook group I am part of, called 'Magnar Istrian' (in Istrian–Venetian dialect this translates to 'eating the Istrian way'). Rather than getting a definitive response, there seemed to be a multitude of names for the shape: *brinsici, puzize, sbirici, maccheroni, makaruni* and even *sorzi nudi* (naked mice!) – variations depending on what town or village your family was from.

Istrian pasta is typically eaten with a rich ragù with ox meat or chicken, but I love to serve it with a pesto-like sauce with thin asparagus spears, walnuts and mint. If you can get your hands on some Istrian olive oil, that would go down even better, as would a glass of chilled Istrian Malvasia wine as an accompaniment.

Hand-rolled macaroni with asparagus, walnuts & mint
(Macaruni con pesto di asparagi)

Serves 4

For the pasta

400 g (2⅔ cups) '00' pasta flour,
   plus extra for dusting
sea salt and freshly cracked
   black pepper
boiling water
200 g (7 oz) thin asparagus
   spears
iced water
75 g (¾ cup) walnuts, processed
   to a coarse crumb
1 small garlic clove, crushed
20 mint leaves, chopped, plus
   extra to garnish
90 ml (3 fl oz) extra virgin olive
   oil, plus extra for serving
40 g (1½ oz) parmesan

To make the pasta, place the flour in a large bowl and add a good pinch of salt. Give it a quick whisk to combine. Next you will need hot water in a pouring jug; I usually mix equal quantities of boiling water and tap water, and find you need about 240 ml (8 fl oz). Slowly pour the hot water into the flour, while mixing it in with a large spoon. When you have added most of the hot water, start using your hands to bring the dough together. The dough should not be sticky, and should come together quite easily to form a firm ball. Add more hot water or flour until you have the right consistency.

Lightly flour your work surface and tip out the dough. Knead the dough for about 8 minutes, or until it is smooth and stretchy. Place in a bowl, cover with a clean tea towel and let it rest for about 30 minutes.

To shape the macaroni – with floured hands, break off a hazelnut-sized ball of the rested dough and roll the ball between your palms, to make an elongated rope that is fatter in the middle and pointy at each end. Repeat until you have rolled out all the macaroni. Cover with a clean tea towel until needed.

Tim the woody ends off the asparagus, reserving them to flavour the stock. Bring a large saucepan of salted water to the boil and add both the woody ends and the trimmed asparagus. Simmer for 5–7 minutes (depending on the thickness of the spears), until they are tender. Using tongs, remove the asparagus spears and plunge into a bowl of iced water. Drain and set aside. Remove and discard the woody ends from the water. Reserve 2 tablespoons of the cooking water to use in the sauce, and keep the rest in the pan to cook the pasta in.

Cut the tips off the asparagus spears and set aside for serving.

Pat the remaining asparagus dry, chop into small pieces, removing any stringy pieces, and place in a food processor. Add the walnuts, garlic, mint and olive oil and pulse until it comes together. Add the parmesan, adjusting the consistency with the reserved asparagus cooking water, and pulse until you have a thick but pourable paste. Add salt and pepper to taste. Set aside.

Bring the reserved asparagus cooking water to the boil, topping up with water if needed. Drop in the macaroni and bring back to the boil. Cook for about 4 minutes, or until cooked to your liking, tossing in the reserved asparagus tips at the last minute to heat through. Drain the lot in a colander.

Pour the asparagus sauce into a large heatproof bowl. Toss in the drained pasta mixture and stir well until evenly coated.

Serve on individual warmed plates, drizzling over a bit more olive oil if desired, and garnishing with a scattering of mint.

Fusi (or *fuži*) are the typical pasta of Istria. Their shape can be one of two: either an equilateral triangle, folded over the end of a wooden spoon, so it looks a bit like origami, or a square that is rolled onto the same wooden spoon, and ends up looking like a delicate tube with sharp angles on the ends, a bit like penne, or smooth Tuscan *garganelli*. The latter are a much more common shape and are so much easier to make.

Online recipes for the dough vary, from having flour mixed just with eggs, to the inclusion of white wine, water or oil (or a combination). The *fusi* I have eaten in Istria are pale, with very little egg in the dough. Whatever ingredients you use, the shape is the important part. I use the handle of my narrowest wooden spoon to make them. A trimmed wooden dowel would also work.

Fusi are typically eaten with a *sugo* containing chicken, hare, partridge or other game, or with truffles. I love them with any sauce that you would eat with pasta, and I usually opt for a simple vegetarian one, made from pantry ingredients.

Fusi with peas, tomatoes & cinnamon
(Fusi coi bisi, pomodoro e cannella)

Serves 4

For the pasta

400 g (2⅔ cups) '00' pasta flour
2 eggs
1 teaspoon extra virgin olive oil
1 tablespoon white wine
80–100 ml (2¾–3½ fl oz) tepid
    or room-temperature water
superfine semolina, for dusting

For the sauce

½ brown onion, finely diced
2–3 tablespoons extra virgin
    olive oil
sea salt and freshly cracked
    black pepper
1 garlic clove, finely diced
600 g (1 lb 5 oz) good-quality
    whole peeled tinned tomatoes
200 g (1½ cups) frozen baby
    peas
¼ teaspoon ground cinnamon
1 handful of parsley leaves,
    chopped
grated parmesan, to serve

Make the pasta dough following the instructions on page 252, using the ingredients at left. Roll out your pasta dough until it is thin, but not too thin – usually the third-last setting on your pasta machine.

Using a large knife, carefully cut the pasta sheets into 5–7 cm (2–2¾ in) squares. I vary the size of the squares depending on the width of the pasta sheet, so that I don't waste too much pasta. As long as they are all the same, it doesn't really matter. Many people make smaller *fusi*, with a 4 cm (1½ in) edge, but I prefer them a bit larger. Dust the squares with semolina as you stack them, then cover with a clean tea towel or napkin before you start rolling.

With your dowel or narrow wooden spoon handle, roll up a square of pasta from one corner, making sure you do not roll it too tightly. It should loosely wrap around the dowel, and the opposite point of the square should now be pressing lightly on the centre of the pasta roll. Press the corner down quite firmly so that it sticks. You should not need water to seal the pasta tube. Cover the prepared *fusi* with a clean tea towel or napkin while you roll out the rest of your pasta.

To make the sauce, place the onion and olive oil in a large frying pan over medium–low heat. Add a pinch of salt and cook for about 10 minutes. Add the garlic and, when fragrant, add the tomatoes plus 60 ml (¼ cup) of water. Simmer for about 20 minutes, then add the peas. Cook for a further 5 minutes or so, until the peas are cooked through. Add the cinnamon, salt and pepper to taste, and stir in half the parsley.

Drop the *fusi* into a large saucepan of salted boiling water and cook until just before done to your liking – this will only take a couple of minutes, depending on the thickness of your pasta.

Drain the pasta, reserving a few tablespoons of the cooking water. Toss the drained pasta in the sauce and stir through, adding a bit of the reserved pasta cooking water if the sauce is a bit too thick.

Serve immediately, sprinkled with the remaining parsley and plenty of parmesan.

Ninetta was in primary school when World War II ended. Over a cup of strong stovetop coffee in her kitchen near Pola/Pula, she told me her post-war story, of why she remained in Pola when all her friends left. 'My grandfather was sick,' she said in the Istrian–Venetian dialect of my father, 'so mamma had to stay behind to nurse him, as did we.' The buildings, the houses, stayed the same, as did life in the family home – but outside those walls, everything was different. Her mother told her not to speak Italian or dialect while in the street for fear of being overhead. Classes at her school were held in a different language, one she did not yet understand. Ninetta said that times were hard, but eventually, the family formed a niche for themselves in the new Pola. Their home and the warmth of the kitchen was their sanctuary and their community.

When I asked if she made her own pasta, she pulled bags of frozen pasta from the freezer: ravioli and traditional *fusi* (squares of pale pasta rolled up diagonally so they resembled penne). Ninetta's ravioli were filled with ricotta, parmesan and a fresh local sheep's milk cheese. I was planning to go back to Pola in 2020 to reconnect with Ninetta and taste her ravioli, but the worldwide pandemic stopped all international travel.

So rather than guess the taste of Ninetta's ravioli, I decided to fill my Istrian-inspired ravioli with greens, based on a *ravioli di verdure* recipe by Mady Fast. The pasta is rolled very thin, so that the filling is clearly visible through the pasta, making them delicious green bites of goodness.

I am looking forward to my next trip to Istria; Ninetta's kitchen will be one of the first places on my list.

Ravioli with greens
(Ravioli di verdure)

**Serves 4 as a starter
(makes 28–32 ravioli)**

For the pasta

125 g (4½ oz) '00' pasta flour
1 large egg
superfine semolina, for dusting

For the filling

1 bunch of English spinach
½ bunch of silverbeet (Swiss
    chard), thick stalks removed
1 small egg, lightly beaten
2 tablespoons sour cream
    or Greek-style yoghurt
zest of ½ lemon
¼ teaspoon freshly grated
    nutmeg
1 heaped tablespoon fine dry
    breadcrumbs, preferably
    homemade
sea salt and freshly cracked
    black pepper

To finish

100 g (3½ oz) unsalted butter
grated parmesan

Make the pasta dough following the instructions on page 252, using the ingredients at left.

While the dough is resting, make your filling. Rinse the spinach several times, removing any thick or damaged stalks. Place a large saucepan over medium–high heat. Add the rinsed spinach (no need to drain) and allow to wilt, using tongs to push the spinach into the base of the pan. Remove the wilted spinach and place in a colander, set over a bowl, to cool and drain. Strain the liquid that collects in the bowl through a fine sieve or muslin (cheesecloth) and reserve this concentrated spinach stock for another use (such as a stock, soup, stew or spinach risotto). Once the spinach has cooled, squeeze it dry by placing it in a clean tea towel and twisting it so that any remaining excess liquid drains out. Finely chop the spinach; you will need about 140 g (5 oz).

Rinse the silverbeet leaves several times, shake the water off and roughly chop. Bring a large saucepan of water to the boil and drop in the silverbeet. Cook for a couple of minutes, or until it has softened. Drain in a colander until it cools, then squeeze it really well in the same tea towel you used for the spinach. Finely chop using a sharp knife or mini food processor. You will need about 110 g (4 oz) finely chopped silverbeet.

Place the silverbeet and spinach in a bowl. Add the egg, sour cream or yoghurt, lemon zest, nutmeg, breadcrumbs, salt and plenty of pepper to taste. Mix well and set aside until ready to use. It should be a fairly dry mix; if any liquid drains out while it is resting, drain it off.

Roll out your pasta dough until it is quite thin – usually the last or second-last setting of your pasta machine.

Using an 8 cm (3¼ in) diameter ravioli cutter or cookie cutter, cut circles of dough. Place a heaped teaspoon of filling in the centre of each circle, leaving a clear edge where you will be able to fold the circle in half. Seal with a bit of water, using your fingertip to apply it around the filling. Press down so that you do not incorporate any air. Repeat until you have used up all the filling and dough, covering them with a tea towel as you go. (At this point I would not allow them to sit for more than a couple of hours.)

Bring a large saucepan of salted water to the boil and cook the ravioli for 3–4 minutes or until the pasta has cooked to your liking.

Meanwhile, in a large frying pan that will fit the ravioli, melt the butter over medium–low heat. Do not let it turn brown. Using a large slotted spoon, transfer the cooked ravioli to the melted butter; don't worry too much if a bit of water drops into the pan. Toss for a minute or two.

Serve on warmed plates, scattered with plenty of parmesan and black pepper.

In my search for ancestors in Istria, I found that the Bacchia surname is firmly embedded in towns a few kilometres from the eastern coast, near the town of Albona/Labin. It is, however, a rare surname. To complicate matters, after World War II, many changed their surnames to Bačić or Baća. My distant cousin Tara, pop singer and resident of Cittanova/Novigrad, found me via social media. Her *nonna* Onorina is 92 and her maiden name was Bacchia; she was also born a few kilometres from the town in which my grandfather was born. We searched for common ancestors in family trees and considered a DNA test. Our scientific ties may be tenuous, but the cultural ones are strong. Tara speaks Croatian as well as Istrian–Venetian dialect and cooks the same food. One day she sent me photos of her *nonna* Onorina and an image of her beautiful *krafi*, which she still makes by hand, served with a meat ragù.

Krafi are a bit like ravioli; this version is traditionally served at weddings. The filling may seem a bit unusual, but the sweetness is not overpowering, and adds a wonderful balance to the salty parmesan. I like to serve them with melted butter and plenty of grated parmesan. They are absolutely delicious!

Onorina's krafi with ricotta
(Krafi di Nonna Onorina)

Serves 4 as a starter (makes 24–26 ravioli)

1 x quantity Egg pasta (page 252)
sea salt

For the filling

45 g (1½ oz) sultanas (golden raisins)
30 ml (1 fl oz) grappa
200 g (7 oz) ricotta, drained
100 g (1 cup) grated parmesan
1 egg, lightly beaten
zest of 1 small lemon
20 g (¾ oz) sugar
20 g (¾ oz) dry breadcrumbs

To serve

melted unsalted butter
plenty of grated parmesan

To make the filling, soak the sultanas in the grappa for at least 2 hours. The sultanas should have absorbed most of the grappa; if not, drain and reserve the grappa for another use (such as in your coffee!).

Place all the filling ingredients, except the breadcrumbs, in a bowl and stir until homogenous. Add as much of the breadcrumbs as you need to make a thick paste; this will depend on how wet your ricotta is. Set aside while you finish making the pasta.

Roll out your pasta dough until it is thin – usually the third-last setting of your pasta machine. The pasta used to make *krafi* is a little thicker than what you would use to make regular ravioli.

To assemble – cut circles of dough using a 9 cm (3½ in) diameter ravioli cutter or cookie cutter. Place a heaped teaspoon of filling in the centre of each circle, leaving a clear edge to fold the circles in half. Seal with a bit of water, using your fingertip to apply it around the filling. Press down so that you do not incorporate any air. Decorate the edges using the tines of a fork.

Bring a large saucepan of salted water to the boil and cook the *krafi* for about 7 minutes, or until the pasta is cooked to your liking. Serve topped with melted butter and plenty of grated parmesan.

Mussels attach themselves to rocks, and the Istrian coastline abounds with them. In beaches with rocky outposts in Port Phillip Bay in Melbourne, especially prior to the 1980s, there were also plenty of them. Finding nests of *peoci*, as my father called them, attached to large rocks just off the shore at low tide was exciting. Prising them off the rocks, less so. For me, scrubbing off barnacles and debearding them was the worst part, but my father did not seem to mind – foraging for food is meant to involve at least a bit of work.

Spaghetti with mussels
(Spaghetti coi peoci)

Serves 2 generously

1 kg (2 lb 3 oz) live mussels
60 ml (¼ cup) olive oil
60 ml (¼ cup) dry white wine, plus extra if needed
200 g (7 oz) dried spaghetti
1 large garlic clove, finely chopped
1 handful of parsley leaves, finely chopped, plus extra to serve
2 tablespoons dry breadcrumbs
sea salt (if needed) and freshly cracked black pepper

Debeard the mussels and scrub off any barnacles under running water. Discard any mussels with broken shells, or any that are open and do not close when you give the shell a hard tap. Place the cleaned mussels in a large bowl, cover with a clean damp tea towel and place in the fridge until ready to use.

In a large frying pan that will fit all the mussels, heat 1 tablespoon of the olive oil over high heat. Add the mussels and the wine and cover, giving the pan an occasional shake. Check every few minutes and lift out the mussels as they open. Any that remain unopened after about 5 minutes should be discarded.

Strain the liquid in the pan through muslin (cheesecloth) to remove impurities. Reserve 170 ml (⅔ cup) of the liquid; if you have less than this, top it up with more dry white wine.

Remove the mussels from their shells, saving a few for decoration. Divide the mussel meat between two bowls. Finely chop the contents of one bowl, and leave the mussels in the other bowl whole.

Cook the spaghetti in a large saucepan of boiling water, according to the packet instructions; I generally don't salt the water, as mussels can be quite salty.

While the pasta is cooking, make the sauce. Place a large frying pan over medium heat. Add the remaining oil, the garlic and half the parsley and cook until fragrant. Add the chopped mussels, the breadcrumbs and the reserved cooking liquid. Cook for a few minutes over low heat, then cover, adjust for salt (you may not need any, as mussels are usually quite salty) and keep warm.

A minute before the spaghetti is cooked to your liking, add the reserved whole mussels and the rest of the parsley to the sauce and season with black pepper.

Drain the spaghetti and add to the sauce. Toss for about a minute, until the sauce coats the spaghetti, then divide between two plates and serve garnished with the reserved mussel shells and extra parsley.

A GET-TOGETHER INVARIABLY INVOLVED CARD GAMES

All our *istriani* friends were card players, and a get-together invariably involved card games. It went something like this:

The men (*i omini*) would be in one room – usually a dining room that had a large table. There would be a pack of cards, *le Triestine*, colourful Italian playing cards in a pack of 40 with images of clubs as giant sticks (*bastoni*), cups (*coppe* that look like chalices), swords and coins. The men, up to four, would play games such as *tresette* or *briscola*. The ones who were not playing would get involved too, standing behind the players, to see what cards they had and cheer them on, or decry the card that had just been played, believing it to be a bad move. The door to the room would be closed to contain the cigarette smoke and the noise, although it didn't do either very well. There were occasional shouts – exclamations rather than words – and swearing, usually in Istrian–Venetian dialect, but sometimes in Croatian (they didn't know much Croatian, except for the curses), followed by calls to the women for more food or wine: 'Liviaaaaa', my father would call out, *'gavemo fame, portine de mangiar'* ('Livia, we're hungry, bring us some food'). It was not a question; it was a call to action.

The women (*le donne*), would be in the kitchen. They would be preparing food, or have set the food out on the kitchen table, waiting for the call. They would be chatting, or playing their own card game – *ramino* (gin rummy), or its variant *scala 40*, with regular cards – occasionally chastising their husbands in the other room for being too loud or swearing or smoking too much.

Upon hearing the call, the ladies would scoop up the platters and enter the men's domain, waving away the clouds of smoke. They would clear the empty glasses to make space for the trays of salami, prosciutto, cheese, olives, pickled vegetables, fried sardines, baked mussels and bread. The next request was, of course, for more wine.

As we say, or rather sing, in dialect: '*Ancora un litro de quel bon*' ('Another litre of the good stuff').

Quando se riunivimo,
giogavimo le carte

This wintery dish is a warming favourite of everyone from *nonni* (grandparents) to the youngest of children. *Gnocchi de gries* are dumplings made from semolina, butter, eggs and cheese, which are cooked in a broth, expanding and soaking up the delicious flavours. I like to put lemon zest in the gnocchi dough, which is not traditional, but gives a lovely balanced taste. I use home-made chicken broth for this dish, but feel free to use my recipe for Really good vegetable stock (page 244) for a vegetarian version.

Semolina gnocchi in broth
(Gnocchi de gries)

Serves 3–4 as a starter

1 egg, separated
sea salt
40 g (1½ oz) unsalted butter, at room temperature
60 g (½ cup) semolina
25 g (¼ cup) grated parmesan, plus extra to serve, if desired
¼ teaspoon ground or grated nutmeg
zest of ½ small lemon
1.25 litres (43 fl oz) good-quality chicken stock (preferably homemade)

In a bowl, whisk the egg white and a pinch of salt until medium peaks form. Set aside.

Place the egg yolk, butter, semolina, parmesan, nutmeg and lemon zest in a bowl. Mix with a spoon for several minutes, or until well combined; the mixture will be fairly dry. In batches, carefully fold in the whisked egg white until well combined. Add salt to taste.

Place the stock in a large saucepan over medium heat and add salt to taste. Bring to the boil, then reduce to a simmer.

Use two teaspoons to help you shape heaped teaspoons of the semolina mixture into small quenelles. They do not need to be perfect; this is a rustic dish. Carefully drop the quenelles into the broth as you make them. They increase in size as they cook and absorb the broth, so don't make them too big.

Once you have made all the dumplings and they are in the broth, simmer for a further 10 minutes, or until they are firm, plump and cooked through.

Serve immediately in small soup bowls, with a little of the broth and extra parmesan if you like.

Driving from the town of Buie/Buje, heading to the south-east, the hilltop town of Montona/Motovun appears as if in an old-style fable. It is often shrouded in mist, with only the very top of it peeking through. And perhaps the forests surrounding Montona are enchanted, if you believe that the edible odd-shaped balls found under the ground near oak trees are the stuff of magic. There is a thriving truffle industry in central Istria, with both the highly prized white and black truffles being available for a large part of the year.

If you have bought truffles before, you will know that they are pricey, but a little goes a long way. They have an unparalleled earthiness that sings of something deep and mystical when you take a sniff of one (or of a container in which one has been stored), and they are best used in a simple dish with eggs, pasta, rice or gnocchi. A less expensive but reasonable substitute for truffles is truffle oil, which you can find in a reputable delicatessen.

Baked gnocchi with taleggio & truffle
(Gnocchi al forno con taleggio e tartufi)

Serves 4

1 x quantity of Potato gnocchi (page 248)
125 g (4½ oz) taleggio, rind removed
150 ml (5 fl oz) pouring (single/ light) cream
60 ml (¼ cup) milk
sea salt and freshly cracked black pepper
unsalted butter, for greasing
1 handful of grated parmesan
fresh black or white truffle, for shaving – or truffle oil, for drizzling

When you have finished preparing the gnocchi, but before cooking them, chop the taleggio into small pieces and place in a small saucepan with the cream and milk over low heat. You want the cheese to melt slowly as the milk and cream warm through. Give it the occasional stir until the cheese has melted completely, about 15 minutes. Add salt and pepper to taste.

Preheat the oven to 200°C (400°F) fan-forced. Grease the base and sides of a 20 cm x 30 cm (8 in x 12 in) baking dish with a little butter.

As the cheesy sauce is cooking, bring a large saucepan of salted water to the boil. Cook the gnocchi, in batches if needed, for a couple of minutes, or until they rise to the surface (more detailed instructions are on page 248).

Using a large slotted spoon, carefully transfer the gnocchi to the baking dish in a single layer. Pour the creamy taleggio sauce over the top, then scatter with a handful of parmesan – don't add too much or it will overpower the dish.

Bake on the top shelf of the oven for about 8 minutes, or until the parmesan has melted and is turning golden.

Top with as much shaved truffle as you like (or as much as you have), or else a good drizzle of truffle oil. Spoon the gnocchi and cheese sauce onto warmed serving plates and serve immediately.

This dish is inspired by one served in one of my favourite Melbourne restaurants, Ragusa. Every time I go there I order this dish. Coloured by cuttlefish ink, the gnocchi are jet black and served with garlicky calamari rings. Another thing I love about this restaurant is that the owner, Sasha, gets out a bottle of grappa (or two) to taste after the meal and will even join you for a drink. I love this level of hospitality, which feels so very European.

Black gnocchi with calamari
(Gnocchi al nero con calamari)

Serves 4 as a starter

For the gnocchi

600 g (1 lb 5 oz) floury old
  potatoes for gnocchi (king
  edward, desiree or red
  potatoes; see page 248)
½ egg, lightly beaten
1 teaspoon cuttlefish ink
100 g (⅔ cup) plain (all-purpose)
  flour, plus extra if needed

For the calamari

450 g (1 lb) cleaned calamari
sea salt
2 tablespoons extra virgin
  olive oil
1 garlic clove, finely diced
good pinch of chilli flakes
1 handful of parsley leaves,
  finely chopped
60 ml (¼ cup) dry white wine

Follow the instructions on page 248 to prepare the gnocchi, using the quantities at left. Incorporate the cuttlefish ink at the same time as the egg.

Prepare the calamari. I like cutting the tube-like body of the calamari into rings (not too thick), the wings into diagonal strips and separating the individual tentacles, cutting the longest ones in half. However, it does depend on the size of the calamari and your preference. Set aside the chopped calamari pieces.

Bring a large (wider rather than deep) saucepan of salted water to the boil.

Place the olive oil in a large non-stick frying pan over medium heat. Add the garlic, chilli flakes and half the parsley. Allow to sizzle for a minute, then drop in the calamari pieces. Increase the heat to medium–high and cook for a minute, then pour in the wine. Allow the wine to evaporate for another minute or so, stirring frequently, then set aside while you boil the gnocchi.

Using a slotted spoon, carefully drop the gnocchi into the boiling water – it should be at a slow rolling boil, not a vigorous one. Do not overcrowd the pan, and have a slotted spoon ready to drain and lift out the gnocchi as they rise to the surface after a minute or two, indicating that they are cooked.

Place the calamari back over medium heat and carefully place the cooked gnocchi in the sauce. Gently toss to combine, scatter with the remaining parsley and serve immediately, on warmed plates.

It might seem odd to match sweet cherries with potatoes, but it is traditional throughout the former Hapsburg lands. Seasonal stone fruit – plums, apricots or cherries – are wrapped in a layer of cooked mashed potatoes, much like a mixture used to make potato gnocchi, then shaped into a ball and gently boiled so the fruit softens. They are then tossed in a buttery sauce with breadcrumbs, cinnamon and sugar. It is a much loved dish for children and adults alike, and is served as a first course, not a dessert. The addition of orange in this recipe with cherries is not traditional, but adds a balancing acidic element to the dish, which is frankly delicious.

If you do not have seasonal stone fruit, you could use your favourite thick jam as a filling.

Potato dumplings with cherries, orange & cinnamon
(Gnocchi di ciliege)

Serves 4 as a starter

For the gnocchi

400 g (14 oz) floury old potatoes
½ small egg (25 g/1 oz) by
   weight), lightly beaten
10 g (¼ oz) unsalted butter,
   at room temperature
sea salt
90–110 g (3–4 oz) plain
   (all-purpose) flour
12 large fresh cherries, pitted
½–1 teaspoon sugar (optional)

For the breadcrumbs

100 g (3½ oz) unsalted butter
4 heaped tablespoons dry
   breadcrumbs
4 teaspoons sugar

To finish

60 ml (¼ cup) freshly squeezed
   orange juice
ground cinnamon, for
   sprinkling
zest of 1 small orange

Follow the cooking process for the potatoes on page 248. Peel the potatoes and place through a potato ricer, or mash very finely. You should have about 300–320 g (10½–11½ oz) of cooked potato. Spread the potato out on your work surface and allow to cool down enough so that you can work with it. The potato should still be slightly warm.

Add the egg and butter and work them through the potato with the tines of a fork. Add a pinch of salt, then about 80 g (2¾ oz) of the flour. Work the dry ingredients into the potato, gently bringing the ingredients together into a dough, as you would for regular gnocchi. Add a bit more of the remaining flour if needed. Do not overwork the dough, or it may absorb more flour than needed, making the dumplings tough or overly doughy.

Clean your work surface and scatter with some of the remaining flour. Roll the potato dough into a thick rope, 5–6 cm (2–2½ in) in diameter. Cut the rope into 12 equal segments, each weighing about 30–32 g (1 oz).

Pat dry your pitted cherries and add a good pinch of sugar to the inside of each cherry where the pip was. You can omit this step if you would prefer a less sweet dish.

Put a segment of potato dough on the palm of one hand, then flatten with your other hand, to form a large disc. Place a cherry inside the disc and wrap the dough carefully around the cherry, so that it is surrounded by an even amount of dough, and forms a ball. Roll the ball on your floured work surface if it feels a bit too sticky or moist. Repeat with the remaining cherries and potato dough.

To cook the dumplings and make the breadcrumbs, you will need to multi-task. Bring a wide saucepan of slightly salted water to the boil. While this is happening, start making your breadcrumbs. Melt the butter in a large non-stick frying pan that will fit all the dumplings over medium–low heat. Once the butter has melted, add the breadcrumbs and allow them to brown slowly, tossing occasionally, for about 5 minutes.

Using a large slotted spoon, carefully drop the dumplings into the boiling water. Reduce the heat a little, but so that the water remains at a rolling boil and cook the dumplings for 4–5 minutes. Do not overcook, or the potato dough may fall apart.

While the dumplings are cooking, continue with the breadcrumbs. Once they are toasted, sprinkle in the sugar and cook for another minute.

Lift the cooked dumplings out of the water with the slotted spoon and carefully drop them into the pan, tossing them gently so they are well coated in the sweet, buttery breadcrumbs.

Serve three dumplings per person on warmed individual plates. Drizzle each serving with a little orange juice, then sprinkle with cinnamon and orange zest. Serve immediately.

Those who live by the sea, especially as children, often grow up with a profound love of seafood. For my father and his Istrian friends in Melbourne – Bibo, Mario and Stanco – fishing and feasting became a big part of their social activities. In the early 1950s, clams (vongole) and mussels were abundant in parts of Port Phillip Bay close to the city. Over the years I heard stories about how all you had to do was stand in knee-deep water and scoop your hand into the sand to find a handful of clams. And this is just what they did, often. Apart from eating clams on their own, just steamed open, we would also have them with spaghetti or risotto.

Risotto with clams
(Risotto alle vongole)

Serves 4

1 kg (2 lb 3 oz) clams or pipis
  (vongole)
sea salt and freshly cracked
  black pepper
3 tablespoons olive oil, plus an
  extra splash
170 ml (⅔ cup) dry white wine,
  such as Malvasia, plus an
  extra splash
2 garlic cloves, peeled
350 g (12½ oz) carnaroli or
  vialone nano rice
4 tablespoons finely chopped
  parsley
2 oil-preserved anchovy fillets,
  chopped (optional)
knob of unsalted butter, to serve

Place the clams in plenty of cold water, with sea salt in the ratio of 1 g salt to every 1 litre (4 cups) water. Leave undisturbed for 4 hours, then drain to remove as much sand as possible from the clams.

Place the clams in a hot frying pan with a lid, in which you have added a trace of olive oil and a splash of white wine. Cover and cook for about 4 minutes, until the clams have steamed open. Place them in a large bowl and cover with an upturned plate, so that the clams will continue to steam and release their juice. Filter the liquid remaining in the pan through fine muslin (cheesecloth) to remove any impurities.

When the clams have cooled down, shell three-quarters of them and keep the rest in their shells. Reserve the liquid in the bowl in which the clams were sitting, filtering it as above and placing it in a small saucepan with the rest of the reserved liquid. Bring the liquid to the boil, topping it up with about 250 ml (1 cup) of water (and more water as needed). Reduce the heat and maintain the broth at a gentle simmer.

Place the olive oil and garlic cloves in a heavy-based saucepan over medium heat. Once the garlic becomes fragrant and starts to turn golden, remove and discard. Add the rice and toast for a few minutes, or until it takes on a slightly golden hue.

Increase the heat, add 125 ml (½ cup) of the wine and stir the rice with a wooden spoon so it does not stick or burn. Once the wine has evaporated, add a ladleful of the warmed clam broth, half the parsley and the anchovy (if using). Stir frequently (though not continuously), adding more hot stock as the previous lot is absorbed by the rice.

The rice will take 15–18 minutes in total to cook through; taste is the best indicator for determining when it is ready. A few minutes before the rice is cooked to your liking, add the shelled clams and the rest of the wine and give it a really good stir for 30 seconds. Season to taste with salt and pepper, and make sure the risotto is not too dry when you remove it from the heat, as the rice will continue to absorb the liquid.

Stir the knob of butter through the rice, then cover and allow to rest for a few minutes.

Serve topped with the reserved clams in their shells, and the remaining parsley.

This red risotto is inspired by a recipe by Francesco Gottardi. He calls it *risotto alla paprica*, with *paprica* referring to the vegetable, rather than the spice. Paprika the spice is common in Hungarian cooking, and is made with roasted capsicums or bell peppers. There are many different kinds of paprika, ranging from sweet to pungent and smoky. I like the sweeter (and more commonly available) varieties, though you could certainly add a bit of the stronger or hotter one to this risotto. For a vegetarian version, omit the pancetta.

Red risotto
(Risotto alla paprica)

Serves 4

1 small brown onion, diced
60 g (2 oz) pancetta, cut into
  5 mm (¼ in) dice
3 tablespoons olive oil
1 red capsicum (bell pepper),
  cut into thin strips about 5 cm
  (2 in) long
boiling water
350 g (12½ oz) risotto rice
  (vialone nano, carnaroli or
  arborio)
125 ml (½ cup) white wine
440 g (15½ oz) tinned chopped
  tomatoes
40 g (1½ oz) unsalted butter
2 teaspoons sweet paprika
½ teaspoon freshly cracked
  black pepper
sea salt
a few handfuls of grated
  parmesan

Place the onion, pancetta and olive oil in a heavy-based saucepan over medium–low heat. The fat on the pancetta will render as it sautés with the onion. After 10 minutes, add the capsicum and continue to cook for another 5 minutes or until the capsicum starts to soften.

Meanwhile, have a kettle or pot of boiling water ready for the next stage.

Add the rice to the saucepan and toast for a few minutes, until it takes on a slightly golden hue. Increase the heat and add the wine, stirring the rice with a wooden spoon so it does not stick or burn. Once the wine has evaporated, add a ladleful of the boiling water. Stir frequently (though not continuously), then add more boiling water as the previous lot is absorbed by the rice – as well as one-quarter of the tomatoes (including their liquid). Keep adding boiling water and the tomatoes in batches as required, stirring frequently. If you run out of tomatoes, just use boiling water.

The rice will take 15–20 minutes in total to cook through; taste is the best indicator for determining when it is ready. A few minutes before the rice is cooked to your liking, add the butter and paprika and give it a really good stir for 30 seconds. Season with the black pepper, and salt to taste, and make sure the risotto is not too dry when you remove it from the heat, as the rice will continue to absorb the liquid.

Stir most of the parmesan through the rice, then cover and allow to rest for a few minutes.

Serve on warmed plates, with extra parmesan on the side.

Savoury pies, strudels & crepes

Torte salate, strudel e palacinche

The influence of the Hapsburgs on food can be seen in the strudels that you will find across much of northern Italy, the Istrian peninsula and down the Dalmatian coast. They are more commonly sweet, but also savoury; the pastry might be an egg pasta dough, a yeasted bread-like dough or a fine olive oil pastry. Fillings of meats, cheeses, vegetables or fruit are spread onto the sheet of dough, then the sheet is rolled up to capture the filling, and left as a long sausage or gently shaped into a spiral. Many strudels are baked, but others are wrapped in a cloth then boiled and, once cooked, sliced and slathered with melted butter.

This version is called *strucolo in straza* in dialect – literally, 'strudel in a cloth'. It is made of egg pasta, and cooked by being immersed in boiling water. This method was used for festive occasions, in particular weddings, when the filling would consist of chicken, pork, ham and sausages. The more common version would be spinach or potatoes and peas.

My version with peas and pancetta is inspired by Annetta in Iolanda de Vonderweid's recipe book. You will need a very large rectangular pan to cook the *strucolo* flat; I use a fish pan. Others join up the two ends of the strudel to make a kind of circle that is cooked by being lowered into a large deep pot, attached by a long string to a strong wooden spoon that sits across the top of the pot. Whichever method you choose, the strudel should be fully immersed in water while it cooks.

Pasta strudel with peas & pancetta
(Strucolo in straza con piselli e pancetta)

Serves 4

For the pasta

250 g (1⅔ cups) '00' pasta flour,
  plus extra, for dusting
2 eggs
2–3 tablespoons water

For the filling

125 g (4½ oz) pancetta,
  finely diced
15 g (½ oz) unsalted butter
1 tablespoon olive oil
1 garlic clove, thinly sliced
500 g (1 lb 2 oz) frozen
  baby peas
sea salt and freshly cracked
  black pepper
60 ml (¼ cup) Béchamel sauce
  (page 233)

To serve

100 g (3½ oz) unsalted butter,
  melted
a few handfuls of grated
  parmesan

Make the pasta following the method on page 252, but using the ingredients at left.

While the pasta is resting, make the filling. Place the pancetta in a large frying pan with the butter and olive oil. Cook over medium–low heat for about 5 minutes, or until the pancetta renders its fat. Add the garlic and sauté until fragrant, then add the peas. Cover and braise for about 30 minutes over low heat, until the peas are well cooked and soft, adding a bit of water as needed. Add salt and pepper to taste. Set aside to cool while you roll out the pasta.

Roll out your pasta dough until it is thin – usually the second-last setting of your pasta machine. To make a large pasta sheet, you will need to join the sheets together, using a little water to seal the edges together. You will need a rectangle of pasta measuring about 30 cm x 50 cm (12 in x 20 in). Alternatively, if you are an experienced pasta maker, you can roll out the whole lot by hand until you have a single rectangle of dough the same size.

Dust a large clean tea towel of the same size with extra flour. Lift the rectangle of dough onto the tea towel. Spread a thin layer of béchamel sauce over the dough, leaving a 10 cm (4 in) wide border on one short edge and a 2 cm (¾ in) border around the other edges. Spoon the cooled pancetta and pea filling over the sauce.

Using the tea towel to help you, carefully lift one short edge so that the pasta rectangle slowly rolls onto itself, towards the 10 cm (4 in) free edge of pasta. Some of the peas may spill out of the sides as you roll the pasta sheet; if so, stop and lift them back onto the pasta sheet. The roll will need to be fairly tight so that the filling stays in place. Secure the ends tightly with kitchen string or elastic bands. Loosely secure the middle of the cloth-covered roll, in three or four places.

Fill a large 35 cm (14 in) wide saucepan with water and bring to the boil, adding a large pinch of salt. Carefully lower the cloth roll into the water using tongs. Once the water comes back to the boil, simmer for 40 minutes.

Carefully remove the roll from the pan and place on a wire rack to drain. Undo the kitchen string and lift the cooked pasta roll onto a chopping board.

Cut into 3–4 cm (1¼–1½ in) thick slices. Carefully lift the slices using a spatula and arrange on individual warmed plates, or a serving platter. Surround the slices with any filling that has dropped out.

To serve, spoon melted butter over the top and scatter with parmesan.

I STOP TO BUY A HANDFUL OF CHERRIES AND A VELVETY APRICOT

Early morning is the best time to visit the market in Pola, before the shoppers, when the fishermen and vegetable sellers are arriving to set up their stalls for the day's trade. Crates full of bream, prawns (shrimp), sardines, calamari, cuttlefish and mussels, cleaned and caught overnight, are hauled into the downstairs hall, on the northern end of the building. The southern end of the hall is for meats, fresh and cured, and delicatessens selling cheeses and smoked meats. Even if you do not know which end is which, once you enter the hallway, the strong aroma will lead you to the one you are looking for.

The market hall was built in the early 1900s, and postcards from the era call it *il mercato nuovo* (the new market). It is a grand building, with finely decorative wrought-iron gates and railings, wide stairwells and semicircular windows that bring in light and warmth. The top level has cafes and outdoor terraces with tables and chairs. The voices of customers rise above the general market hubbub – Croatian, Istrian–Venetian dialect and the occasional German and English words can be heard from those sipping coffee, beer or grappa and eating pastries. Signs with 'Der markt' and 'Fischmarkt' on the building itself speak to its Hapsburg origins, but the market is very much of the people of Pola.

To the east of the market hall are the fruit and vegetable sellers. Permanent concrete trestles are piled high with the abundance of the season, collected from the market gardens on the outskirts of Pola and of neighbouring towns: artichokes, tomatoes, zucchini (courgettes) flowers, cherries and *radiceto*, the local leafy chicory (endive) used as a salad green. The signs on the produce are in Croatian, and the voices of the older women selling the vegetables, the *donne della verdure*, are a mix of Istrian–Venetian and Croatian; the language they use depends on their customer.

Vertically stacked jars of *med* (honey in Croatian) catch the morning sun, casting a golden halo around wedges of honeycomb. An odd-sized assortment of jars have 'Pula' handwritten on them: local small-batch honey. Leafy chestnut trees and ruby-coloured umbrellas provide welcome shade as the sun rises higher in the hot summer sky, making patches of shadow and light on the market stalls, on the produce, and on the crowds who come to buy the freshest Istrian produce. I stop to buy a handful of cherries, a velvety apricot and a bunch of sunny zucchini flowers to take to Gianna.

My first morning in Pola is always spent at the market, drinking in the smells of the season and the sounds of the community.

*Mi fermo a comprare una manciata
di ciliegie e un'albicocca vellutata*

My favourite savoury strudel is based on a spinach strudel, and baked rather than boiled. In the filling I replace the more traditional ricotta with potatoes. It uses the same super-fine strudel pastry as my Apricot strudel (page 178), and makes a hearty meal with an accompanying salad. You could replace the butter in the pastry with olive oil or a vegan butter for a vegan version of the dish, and brush the pastry with olive oil. As a finishing touch, I love scattering poppy seeds on the dough; this is not essential, but as my mother would say, '*L'ocio ga la sua parte*' ('The eye also plays a role').

Strudel with greens & potatoes
(Strudel de erbete co' le patate)

Serves 4

For the filling

2 mashing potatoes, about 450 g (1 lb)

sea salt and freshly cracked black pepper

3–4 tablespoons extra virgin olive oil

1 large brown onion, finely diced

400 g (14 oz) silverbeet (Swiss chard) or rainbow chard, thick stalks removed

400 g (14 oz) English spinach or baby spinach

50 g (1¾ oz) unsalted butter, melted

2 tablespoons fine dry breadcrumbs

a good handful of grated parmesan (optional)

To make the filling, peel the potatoes and cut each into about six pieces. Place in a saucepan filled with cold water, add a good pinch of salt and bring to the boil. Cook, covered, until fork-tender. Drain and set aside.

Meanwhile, place the olive oil in a small saucepan over medium–low heat. Add the onion, with a pinch of salt, and cook slowly for about 20 minutes, or until the onion is soft, sticky and just starting to caramelise. Add the cooked potato and stir through with a fork, mashing as you go – the potato only needs to be roughly mashed. Add salt and pepper to taste. Set aside to cool.

Cut the silverbeet leaves into thin strips and roughly chop the spinach. Blanch them in a saucepan of salted boiling water, then drain well and set aside to cool. Taste once cooled to ensure they are sufficiently salted.

To make the pastry, place the flour in a bowl with a pinch of salt, giving it a good whisk to combine. Make a well in the centre and add 105 ml (3½ fl oz) of water and the butter. Stir with a spoon until well combined. Tip the dough onto a well-floured work surface and knead initially with your fingertips, until it no longer sticks to your fingers, and then with the heel of your hand for at least 10 minutes. Don't be tempted to add extra flour – the dough will end up very smooth, soft and supple. Place in a clean bowl, cover with an upturned plate and leave to rest for 30 minutes.

Preheat the oven to 160°C (320°F) fan-forced.

Place a clean tablecloth on a flat surface and dust with flour, ready for rolling the dough.

For the pastry

180 g (1¼ cups) plain (all-
    purpose) flour, plus extra
    for dusting
sea salt
30 g (1 oz) unsalted butter,
    softened

To finish

1 egg yolk, beaten with a dash
    of milk (or just milk)
1 tablespoon poppy seeds

To roll out the pastry dough, dust your work surface with extra flour and gently roll the dough into a rectangle, flipping it over regularly and dusting with more flour as you go, so the delicate pastry does not stick and tear.

Once the dough is about 30 cm x 40 cm (12 in x 16 in), carefully lift it onto the floured tablecloth.

Finish stretching the dough by hand, by carefully placing your hands under the pastry sheet and gently stretching any sections that look thicker. Your sheet needs to be at least 50 cm x 60 cm (20 in x 24 in). If it is any smaller than this, you haven't stretched it thinly enough – you should be able to easily read through the dough. When you are ready to assemble the strudel, turn the dough so a longer edge is facing you. Trim any thick edges and discard.

Brush the dough with the melted butter. Scatter the breadcrumbs over the bottom one-third of the dough, leaving a 4 cm (1½ in) border free at each end. The other two-thirds of the pastry should have no breadcrumbs. Evenly scatter the cooled greens over the breadcrumbs, then the mashed potato, and finally the parmesan (if using).

Starting from the edge of pastry that has the filling, use the tablecloth to help you roll the strudel into a long sausage enclosing the filling, a little bit at a time, taking care not to roll it too tightly. When the strudel has been rolled completely, roll it in on itself to form a spiral and carefully slide it onto a large sheet of baking paper.

Transfer the strudel and baking paper to a 24 cm (9½ in) pie dish. Brush the outer surface of the pastry with the egg wash and scatter over the poppy seeds.

Bake for about 55 minutes, or until the top is deep golden. Check halfway through cooking and reduce the oven temperature if the strudel is browning too much.

Wait at least 10 minutes before slicing and serving; the strudel is also lovely at room temperature.

Once cooled, the strudel will keep in an airtight container in a cool spot for a couple of days.

The filling of this savoury cheese strudel is inspired by one in Francesco Gottardi's book about the food of Fiume/Rijeka during the reign of the Hapsburgs. In addition to ricotta, it contains mustard and cumin seeds, giving it a deeply savoury quality that I love. As one of the cheeses, I use spiced gouda, which is studded with cumin seeds. If you cannot find it, use regular gouda and add ½ teaspoon toasted cumin seeds.

Spiced cheese strudel
(Strudel di formaggi)

Serves 8

For the pastry

180 g (1¼ cups) plain
  (all-purpose) flour, plus extra
  for dusting
sea salt
2½ tablespoons extra virgin
  olive oil

For the filling

400 g (14 oz) ricotta, well
  drained
50 ml (1¾ fl oz) pouring (single/
  light) cream
50 g (1¾ oz) Greek-style yoghurt
50 g (½ cup) grated parmesan
125 g (4½ oz) spiced gouda,
  grated
50 g (1¾ oz) unsalted butter,
  at room temperature
2 eggs, separated
2 teaspoons French mustard
sea salt and freshly cracked
  black pepper

To finish

milk, for brushing
grated parmesan, for sprinkling

To make the pastry, place the flour in a bowl with a pinch of salt, giving it a good whisk to combine. Make a well in the centre, add the olive oil and 105 ml (3½ fl oz) of water and stir with a spoon until well combined. Tip the pastry onto a floured work surface and knead initially with your fingertips, until it no longer sticks to your fingers, and then with the heel of your hand for at least 10 minutes. Don't be tempted to add extra flour – the dough will end up very smooth, soft and supple. Place in a clean bowl, cover with an upturned plate and leave to rest for 30 minutes.

To make the filling, place the ricotta in a large bowl and mix with a spoon to smooth out any lumps. Add the cream, yoghurt, parmesan, gouda, butter, egg yolks and mustard. Season with salt and pepper and mix until well combined. The mixture will be quite thick.

Beat the egg whites with a whisk until medium peaks form, then fold through the cheese mixture in batches. Set aside until ready to use.

Preheat the oven to 160°C (320°F) fan-forced.

Place a clean tablecloth on a flat surface and dust with flour, ready for rolling the dough.

To roll out the pastry dough, dust your work surface with extra flour and gently roll the dough into a rectangle, flipping it over regularly and dusting with more flour as you go, so the delicate pastry does not stick and tear.

Once the dough is about 30 cm x 40 cm (12 in x 16 in), carefully lift it onto the floured tablecloth.

Finish stretching the dough by hand, by carefully placing your hands under the pastry sheet and gently stretching any sections that look thicker. Your sheet needs to be at least 50 cm x 60 cm (50 in x 24 in). If it is any smaller than this, you haven't stretched it thinly enough – you should be able to easily read through the dough. When you are ready to assemble the strudel, turn the dough so a shorter edge is facing you. Trim any thick edges and discard.

Spoon the filling over the bottom one-third of the dough. Using the tablecloth to assist you, gently roll the strudel into a long sausage. I kept the strudel straight, but for this you will need a long baking tray and a large enough oven. Alternatively, you can curve the strudel into a horse-shoe shape and lift it onto a lined baking tray.

Bake for 25 minutes, then brush the strudel with milk. Check the pastry isn't browning too quickly; if it is, reduce the oven temperature slightly.

Continue baking for another 20 minutes. Scatter some parmesan over the strudel and bake for another 5 minutes, or until the cheese has melted and is golden, and the pastry is cooked.

Allow to cool slightly before slicing; the strudel is delicious warm or at room temperature. Once cooled, the strudel can be stored in an airtight container in the fridge for a few days.

This vegetarian pie is broadly based on one by Marchesa Eta Polesini and uses what she calls *'la famosa pasta speciale'* (famous special pastry), a forgiving all-purpose pastry that does not need to be blind-baked – which is, she writes, what makes it special. Unlike most types of pastry, baking powder is worked into the dough after it has rested. I vary the original recipe, substituting part of the plain flour with spelt flour, which gives the pastry a nuttier taste and a darker colour. It is a terrific dough that can be rolled very thinly.

The filling uses up those vegetables lurking at the back of the fridge or pantry; feel free to substitute the ones in the recipe below with what you have on hand, as long as the quantities remain roughly the same. Using Marsala as the braising liquid gives the vegetables a lovely sweetness.

Silverbeet & cauliflower vegetable pie
(Torta salata con blede e cavolfiore)

Serves 6–8

For the pastry

250 g (1⅔ cups) plain (all-purpose) flour – or a mix of 200 g (1⅓ cups) plain (all-purpose) flour and 50 g (⅓ cup) spelt flour, plus extra for dusting
sea salt
160 g (5½ oz) chilled unsalted butter, chopped into small dice
2 eggs
1 tablespoons rum (or milk), plus a splash more if needed
2 scant teaspoons baking powder

To make the pastry, use your fingers to rub the flours and a good pinch of salt into the butter, until it resembles wet sand. (You can also use the pulse function on your food processor.) Work in the eggs and rum or milk until you have a smooth, cohesive dough. Roll out into a large disc on a floured work surface, then wrap (I use baking paper) and allow to rest for 1 hour in a cool spot.

To make the filling, finely dice the silverbeet and onion. Place the olive oil and butter in a large frying pan over medium heat. Add the silverbeet and onion and a good pinch of salt and sauté for about 10 minutes without allowing the mixture to brown. While this is happening, chop the cauliflower (including the central spine) into chunks no larger than 1 cm (½ in).

Add the garlic to the pan and cook until fragrant. Next add the cauliflower and peas and allow to warm through, then add the Marsala and increase the heat to medium–high. Cook for a few minutes, then reduce the heat and cover. Cook for about 12 minutes, or until the cauliflower is tender. If there is a lot of liquid in the pan, remove the lid and cook for a few more minutes so the liquid evaporates.

Transfer the mixture to a large bowl and allow to cool. Add the remaining filling ingredients and season with salt and pepper. Mix together and set aside.

For the filling

250 g (9 oz) silverbeet (Swiss chard) or rainbow chard, including the white leaf spine, but not the thick lower stalks
½ white onion, peeled
1 tablespoon extra virgin olive oil
15 g (½ oz) unsalted butter, plus extra for greasing
sea salt and freshly cracked black pepper
½ small cauliflower, about 250 g (9 oz)
1 garlic clove, finely diced
155 g (1 cup) frozen peas
60 ml (¼ cup) Marsala
50 g (½ cup) grated parmesan
2 eggs, lightly beaten
1 tablespoon finely chopped parsley
1 teaspoon white wine vinegar

Preheat the oven to 160°C (320°F) fan-forced. Line the base of a 24 cm (9½ in) tart (flan) tin with baking paper (my tin has a removable base). Carefully rub butter around the side of the tin.

Scatter the baking powder over the ball of dough and knead quickly and vigorously until it is incorporated. Cut off about one-third of the pastry to use as the pie lid; the larger portion will be for the base and side of the pie.

On a lightly floured work surface, roll out the larger dough portion to a circle a little bigger than your tart tin. Drape the dough over the tin and press it down into the side; you should have a small amount of dough overhanging the edge. Spoon the filling into the base.

Roll out the remaining dough to make a pie lid, then drape it over the filling. Seal the pie by rolling the overhanging dough over the pastry lid into a raised crust all around the top of the pie. Use any pastry scraps to cut out shapes to decorate the top of the pie, if you like, and insert a small hole in the centre for steam to escape.

Bake for 50–55 minutes, checking periodically that the pie is not browning too much; if it is, reduce the oven temperature slightly. The pie is cooked when the top is firm and golden.

Place on a wire rack and serve warm, or at room temperature. Once cooled, the pie will keep in an airtight container in the fridge for 3–4 days.

Thin crepes (*palacinche*) are very versatile. In addition to piling on a filling and rolling them up like a cigar, they can also be folded into semicircles or quarters, doused in a sauce or melted butter and overlapped on a baking tray before baking. They can be easily stacked and made into a fancy-looking torte, either savoury or sweet. For a savoury version, Iolanda de Vonderweid suggests spinach, mortadella and béchamel sauce mixed with a meat ragù in alternating layers – a concept I love.

Here I've simplified the ingredients a little, replacing the ragù with a creamy blue cheese. The dish looks complicated, but it is actually quite easy. All of the components can be made the day before, and the stack assembled just before baking, so it is a good dish to prepare when you are entertaining. The béchamel holds everything together, so the coloured layers look quite fancy when they are sliced.

Crepe stack with spinach, ham & blue cheese
(Torta salata di palacinche)

Serves 6–8

1 large bunch of English spinach
25 g (1 oz) unsalted butter
½ teaspoon freshly ground
    nutmeg
sea salt
1 tablespoon dry breadcrumbs
10 Savoury crepes (page 257)
½ x quantity of Béchamel sauce
    (page 233)
100 g (3½ oz) mild creamy blue
    cheese, finely chopped
180 g (6½ oz) thinly sliced
    smoked ham, finely diced
50 g (½ cup) grated parmesan

Rinse the spinach several times, removing any thick or damaged stalks. Place a large saucepan over medium–high heat, add the spinach (no need to drain) and allow to wilt, using tongs to push the spinach into the base of the pan. Transfer the spinach to a colander set over a bowl, to cool and drain. Strain the liquid that collects in the bowl through a fine sieve or muslin (cheesecloth) and reserve this concentrated spinach stock for another use (such as a stock, soup, stew or spinach risotto). You should have about 250 g (9 oz) spinach. Finely chop the spinach using a sharp knife or mini food processor.

Melt 20 g (¾ oz) of the butter in a frying pan over medium heat. Toss the spinach through the butter. Add the nutmeg and salt to taste, and stir through the breadcrumbs. Set aside to cool.

Preheat the oven to 180°C (350°F) fan-forced. Line a baking tray with baking paper.

Place your first crepe on a work surface, then smear it with a generous tablespoon of béchamel. Scatter over one-third of the blue cheese.

Place your second crepe on top. Smear with a generous tablespoon of béchamel, then scatter over one-third of the ham.

Place your third crepe on top. Spoon over one-third of the spinach mixture and scatter with one-third of the parmesan.

Repeat until you have three layers of each of the three fillings. Place the final crepe on top, and brush it with the remaining butter, which should have softened.

Bake for 10 minutes, until the crepes are warmed through and the cheese has melted. The stack will be easier to slice once it has cooled slightly. To do this, transfer the stack, using the baking paper to help you, onto a chopping board. Once it has cooled further, slice into wedges using a sharp wide-bladed knife, cleaning the knife after you make each cut.

This dish is also lovely at room temperature. If you have some left over, store it in the fridge in an airtight container (the ones made for cakes work really well). Take it out of the fridge a few hours before serving to bring it to room temperature.

You can also gently reheat it in the oven for 10 minutes, covering the top with foil to stop it browning too much.

My mother often made 'cannelloni' with crepes rather than pasta, filling them with ricotta, parmesan and spinach. This was one of the first dishes I made for my husband, Mark, before we were married. I like to think it cemented our relationship – although he will probably say it was my mother's apple strudel. This dish was inspired by a recipe by Edda Vidiz and Cesare Fonda, who have written a number of books about traditional cooking in and around Trieste when it was ruled by the Hapsburgs. If you do not like the bitterness of radicchio, you can instead use a big bunch of English spinach, which you will need to blanch first; in this case, omit the olive oil, balsamic vinegar and brown sugar. But I urge you to try this radicchio version. It has a lovely, complex taste.

Crepe cannelloni with radicchio & blue cheese
(Caneloni col radicio)

Serves 4

1 large head of radicchio di Treviso, or 2 small heads, about 350 g (12½ oz)
a good splash of olive oil
2 teaspoons good-quality balsamic vinegar
1 teaspoon brown sugar
sea salt
50 g (1¾ oz) unsalted butter
250 ml (1 cup) Béchamel sauce (page 233)
8 Savoury crepes (page 257)
150 g (5½ oz) creamy blue cheese
1 heaped tablespoon dry breadcrumbs
60 g (2 oz) parmesan, grated

Remove and discard the thick spines from the radicchio leaves. Cut the leaves into strips and wash them. If they are particularly bitter or you do not enjoy too much bitterness, soak them in water for 15 minutes or more, tasting as you go, before draining them.

Place the olive oil in a large frying pan over medium heat. Sautè the radicchio, in batches if needed, for a few minutes, or until starting to wilt. Stir the vinegar through until the radicchio is well coated. Toss in the sugar, stirring until it dissolves. If there is a lot of liquid left in the pan, briefly turn up the heat so it evaporates. Add salt to taste, then set aside to cool.

Preheat the oven to 160°C (320°F) fan-forced. Use a small amount of the butter to grease the base of a large baking dish that will fit all the crepes rolled up; mine measured 24 cm x 28 cm (9½ in x 11 in).

Mix the béchamel through the cooled radicchio mixture. Smear one-eighth of the mixture along one edge of a crepe, then scatter with one-eighth of the blue cheese. Roll up and place in the baking dish. Fill and roll all the remaining crepes in the same way, placing them side by side in your baking dish quite snugly, but not squashed together.

Melt the remaining butter. Evenly scatter the breadcrumbs over the crepes, drizzle with the melted butter and, finally, scatter with the parmesan. Bake for 10 minutes, or until warmed through, then use the oven grill (broiler) setting to brown the cheese topping for a few minutes.

Serve warm, with a green side salad.

Land & sea

Mare e monti

I belong to a Facebook group called 'Magnar Istrian', where Istrian recipes are shared by home cooks and communicated in Istrian–Venetian dialect. When the recipe for *sarme* (the Croatian word for cabbage rolls) was shared, a discussion ensued as to whether these were authentically Istrian, or borrowed from Hungary, Turkey or Serbia. Some commented that their mothers and grandmothers had never made them, though others wrote that they were eaten in Fiume/Rijeka. I agree that these rolls are borrowed; that said, they are something I grew up eating, and my father, Istrian born and bred, loved them.

My mother learned to make her *involtini de verza* (cabbage rolls) from Istrian ladies at social clubs in the 1950s. The filling was a mixture of minced (ground) pork and beef, and rice, and parboiled cabbage leaves were used to wrap the filling. The rolls were placed side by side in the electric frying pan, but not too tightly, as they would expand slightly as they slowly cooked. My sister would ask for these every May, for her birthday lunch. Sadly, Mamma did not write down the recipe, so I have borrowed elements from Francesco Gottardi. He suggests using fermented or sour cabbage leaves, much like sauerkraut, to wrap the filling, giving a slightly sour but well-balanced taste to the dish.

You can buy jars of preserved cabbage leaves from a continental delicatessen, or else approximate the taste of sauerkraut by boiling the cabbage whole in water and vinegar. You will need a large pot that will fit the whole cabbage if you decide to boil your own.

Cabbage rolls
(Involtini de verza)

Makes 12

1 small–medium head of
  cabbage, or a large jar of
  preserved cabbage leaves
sea salt
white wine vinegar (if using
  fresh cabbage leaves)
200 g (7 oz) minced (ground)
  beef
200 g (7 oz) minced (ground)
  pork
80 g (heaped ⅓ cup) short-grain
  or medium-grain rice
1 brown onion, finely diced
1 garlic clove, finely chopped
1 tablespoon finely chopped
  parsley
1 teaspoon sweet paprika
1 teaspoon caraway seeds,
  crushed
3 tablespoons olive oil
70–140 g (½–1 cup) loosely
  packed shredded sauerkraut
400 ml (13½ fl oz) home-made
  beef stock, or other stock or
  water
mustard of your choice, to serve

If using fresh cabbage, bring a large saucepan of salted water to the boil. Add the vinegar in the ratio of 60 ml (¼ cup) to 1 litre (4 cups) water. Remove any dark green damaged leaves from the outside of the cabbage, then turn it over so that the base is facing upwards. With a small paring knife, carefully remove the core – it should be shaped like a cone, wider at the top and narrowing to a point as it gets to the centre of the cabbage head. Carefully lower the cabbage into the boiling water. Once the water returns to the boil, reduce the heat, cover and cook for about 10 minutes. At this point the leaves should be cooked. Carefully remove the cabbage, but reserve the hot water in the pan in case you find that the centre of the cabbage is not quite cooked and you need to simmer it a little longer. Remove the leaves one at a time. Flatten the central spine by trimming the thick bulbous part if it is too thick to roll up, or cut it out of the leaf. You will need 12 cabbage leaves, measuring about 12 cm x 18 cm (4¾ in x 7 in). The pieces should be approximately the same size; you don't need to be too fussy about it, though. Omit this step if using store-bought preserved cabbage leaves – though the spines of these sometimes need to be trimmed as above.

To make the filling, place the following in a large bowl: the beef, pork, rice, onion, garlic, parsley, paprika, caraway seeds and 1 scant teaspoon of salt. Mix well with your hands, until the mixture is homogenous.

Place a 'baton' of filling, about 50 g (1¾ oz), along one end of a cabbage leaf, then roll it up loosely like you would a cigar, folding the ends in slightly. The roll should be about 4 cm (1½ in) thick. Do not roll it up tightly, as the rice will expand as it cooks. Repeat to make 12 rolls.

Drizzle the olive oil into a frying pan with a lid; it should form a thin layer that covers the whole pan. Lay the cabbage rolls in the pan side by side. Place as much shredded sauerkraut as will fit between the rolls, then add enough stock to almost cover the rolls – depending on your pan size, you may not need all the stock, or you may need to top it up with a bit of water. If your pan is a smaller size, or you're making a double quantity, you can layer the rolls on top of each other.

Place over medium heat and bring to the boil, then reduce the heat, cover and simmer slowly for just over 1 hour.

If there is too much liquid in the pan, remove the lid and increase the heat to medium for about 5 minutes, so some of the liquid evaporates. (If you have made a large quantity and you are not eating them all in one sitting, a bit of liquid in the base of the pan is good – use this to keep the rolls moist in a lidded ceramic container in the fridge.)

Serve the cabbage rolls warm, with your favourite mustard. They are delicious with smashed potatoes with onion and olive oil (page 157). They are even better after three or four days.

Stuffed peppers (and tomatoes) have always been a summer dish – for me, at least. Growing up in Australia, while many of my friends might buy lunch or bring white sliced bread sandwiches when they went to the beach, my mother would send me off with a very European packed lunch: if it wasn't a crusty *pasta dura* bread roll with mortadella and emmental, it would be a stuffed pepper, a generous handful of cherries or plums, and a few slices of ricotta cake to share.

Mamma would put rice and minced (ground) meat in the stuffing, very similar to the filling in her cabbage rolls. She would use fat green capsicums (bell peppers), and make stuffed tomatoes at the same time. They jostled for space in the electric frying pan, the tomatoes collapsing a little faster than the firmer-skinned capsicums as they cooked. As she didn't write down the recipe, I approximated one from a local restaurant, Ragusa, where they use narrower banana peppers. They are cooked and served in a rich sauce made with roasted capsicum – dramatically red and just delicious.

Oven-roasted stuffed banana peppers
(Peveroni ripieni)

Makes 8

8 red banana peppers
200 g (7 oz) minced (ground) pork
200 g (7 oz) minced (ground) beef
50 g (¼ cup) short-grain or medium-grain rice
1 small brown onion, grated
1 garlic clove, finely chopped
1 teaspoon sea salt
½ teaspoon sweet paprika
½ teaspoon cumin seeds, crushed
¼ teaspoon hot smoked paprika
1 egg
1 tablespoon chopped parsley
150 ml (5 fl oz) Roasted pepper sauce (page 230)

To prepare the banana peppers, remove the tops and scrape out the seeds and spines using a long-handled small spoon. Rinse and leave to dry upside down.

Preheat the oven to 150°C (300°F) fan-forced.

Place the remaining ingredients, except the roasted pepper sauce, in a bowl and mix well using a spoon or your hands. Stuff the mixture into the peppers, a little bit at a time. Do not overfill, as the rice will swell during cooking.

In a roasting tin that is large enough to fit all the peppers in a single layer, smear a layer of the roasted pepper sauce. Lay the filled peppers on top, then cover with the rest of the sauce and 60 ml (¼ cup) of water. Cover with the foil.

Roast for 30 minutes, then remove the foil and continue to roast for at least another 45 minutes, or until the peppers are nicely roasted and cooked through when pierced with a fork. (I turn the peppers over a few times while they are roasting uncovered, so that their skin colours evenly.)

Allow to cool for at least 10 minutes before serving. There should be quite a bit of sauce in the bottom of the tin to spoon over the peppers.

Serve with polenta 'Isola' style (page 247), smashed potatoes with onion and olive oil (page 157) or crusty bread.

When I was growing up at home, chicken was a dish we ate on a Sunday, a festive dish, roasted whole, or stuffed or made into a ragù to serve with gnocchi. This dish is based on Iolanda de Vonderweid's *pollo all'istriana* (Istrian chicken), which she describes as 'exquisite'. A whole chicken is cut into eight (by your butcher, if you do not want to) and simmered with tomatoes, marjoram and roasted capsicum (bell peppers). I love serving this dish with polenta or potatoes; both do an excellent job of mopping up the colourful sauce.

Chicken with roasted peppers
(Pollo co'i peveroni)

Serves 6–8

1.5 kg (3 lb 5 oz) whole chicken, cut into 8 pieces
sea salt and freshly cracked black pepper
3 tablespoons extra virgin olive oil
1 large brown onion, finely diced
1 garlic clove, sliced
125 ml (½ cup) dry white wine
440 g (15½ oz) tinned peeled tomatoes, diced
1 teaspoon dried marjoram
3 red or yellow capsicums (bell peppers), roasted and skins removed (see page 230)

Lightly rinse the chicken pieces and pat dry. Trim off the excess fat, but keep the skin on. Dust the chicken pieces with salt and pepper and set aside. Make sure the chicken is at room temperature before cooking.

Place the olive oil in a large heavy-based saucepan that will fit the chicken in a single layer. Add the onion and sauté over medium–low heat for about 12 minutes, or until translucent but not yet coloured. Add the garlic and cook until fragrant.

Add the chicken and brown for 8–10 minutes, regularly turning the pieces with tongs so they cook evenly and do not stick to the base of the pan.

Increase the heat and add the wine. Allow it to evaporate for a few minutes, then add the tomatoes (including the juice). Stir through and reduce the heat to medium. Once it starts to simmer, add the marjoram. Reduce the heat to low, cover and simmer for about 25 minutes.

Cut the roasted capsicum into strips, nearly as wide as your finger. Add to the chicken and cook for a further 15–20 minutes, until the chicken is cooked through. Season to taste with salt and pepper.

Serve with polenta 'Isola' style (page 247), warm soft polenta or smashed potatoes with onion and olive oil (page 157).

Goulash is a hearty wintery meal, one I am certain my *nonni* (grandparents) would have enjoyed in their home in Pola/Pula. If you think the dish is Hungarian, you are right, it is. But when my grandfather Matteo was born in Chersano/Kršan in central Istria, it was part of the Austro–Hungarian empire – and with the migration of people come the food traditions.

This is a particularly delicious version, made with sauerkraut, that goes by the name *szekely gulasch*. Most of the books I used to research the old recipes of Istria mention this goulash. It calls for a mix of beef and pork, rather than the more usual Hungarian version with only pork, and marries well with potatoes. Francesco Gottardi suggests crumbling a pre-cooked potato into the stew, but others suggest it be eaten with potato gnocchi – which is exactly how I like it.

Beef & pork goulash with sauerkraut
(Szekely gulasch)

Serves 8–10

60 ml (¼ cup) olive oil

1 large brown onion, finely diced

sea salt

1 large garlic clove, finely sliced

600 g (1 lb 5 oz) pork shoulder,
  cut into 2–3 cm (¾–1¼ in) dice

200 g (7 oz) topside beef, cut into
  2–3 cm (¾–1¼ in) dice

2 tablespoons sweet paprika

1 teaspoon crushed cumin seeds

½ teaspoon crushed caraway
  seeds

½ teaspoon freshly cracked
  black pepper

200 g (7 oz) peeled tinned
  tomatoes

250 ml (1 cup) beef stock,
  preferably home-made

500 g (3½ cups) sauerkraut,
  drained

200 g (7 oz) sour cream, to serve

Place the olive oil in a large flameproof casserole dish over medium–low heat. Add the onion and a pinch of salt and sauté for about 10 minutes, or until the onion is translucent, softened and just starting to brown. Add the garlic and cook until fragrant.

Increase the heat to medium. Brown the pork and beef, stirring regularly; there should still be a bit of pink left when you're done. Add the spices and stir them through, then add the tomatoes and enough stock to just cover the meat. Once it starts simmering, cover and reduce the heat so that it is barely bubbling. Cook for about 1 hour 20 minutes, or until the meat is tender, stirring occasionally

Before adding your sauerkraut, have a taste to see how sour it is. If it is too sour for your taste, rinse it in plenty of cold water and drain well.

Once you are happy with the taste of the sauerkraut, add it to the goulash and cook for another 10 minutes or so. Add salt to taste. Lastly, swirl through the sour cream and serve immediately. (If you are not eating it immediately, I would leave out the sour cream, which should be swirled through just before serving – even on individual plates.)

Serve the goulash with potato gnocchi (page 248) – or if you have less time, mashed potatoes will do fine.

Useleti (or *oseleti*) is a dialect word meaning 'little birds' (in Italian, *uccellini*) – which is what these little meat rolls are meant to resemble. The dish is a Venetian one, from the time when people did eat little birds, stewed in the pan, served with polenta.

Useleti, also called *useleti scampai* ('little birds that have escaped'– though I guess if they are in the pan, they have probably been caught!) are traditionally made with thin slices of veal, layered with slices of cured pork or pancetta and sage leaves, rolled up and then pan-fried in a sauce made of wine, a hint of tomato, and the juices that are released during cooking. I take my inspiration for this recipe from my aunt Dina, who would make a similar version, adding cheese to the filling. Serve with polenta or Smashed potatoes with onion and olive oil (page 157), so you can collect all the delicious pan juices.

Stuffed little meat rolls
(Useleti scampai)

Serves 4

12 slices veal or yearling round-
    eye (girello), about 600 g
    (1 lb 5 oz)
sea salt
12 thin slices pancetta
6 thin slices good-quality
    leg ham, cut in half
12 large sage leaves
60 g (2 oz) gruyère, cut into
    12 batons
3 tablespoons extra virgin
    olive oil
125 ml (½ cup) white wine
60 ml (¼ cup) tomato passata
    (puréed tomatoes)

Ask your butcher to bang out the slices of veal, so they are about 6 cm x 8 cm (2½ in x 3¼ in) in size. Sprinkle with salt. Layer with the pancetta and ham slices, one on top of the other; they should be slightly smaller than the meat. Place a sage leaf and cheese baton on one end – the cheese should be slightly smaller than the length of the meat on the short edge. Roll up and thread with a toothpick so the meat roll is well secured.

Place the olive oil in a frying pan that will fit all the rolls in a single layer (they will shrink slightly) and set over medium–high heat. Add the meat rolls and sear for about 3 minutes on each side, turning frequently, until nicely coloured.

Add the wine, passata and 185–250 ml (¾–1 cup) of water; the rolls should be a bit over halfway covered with liquid. Bring to the boil, then reduce the heat. Cover and simmer for about 30 minutes, turning the rolls every now and then so they are bathed in the pan juices. Remove the lid for the last 10 minutes of cooking to thicken the sauce. The meat should be cooked through and tender after 40–50 minutes.

If there is too much sauce, remove the rolls and place them on a warmed plate, then turn up the heat to reduce the sauce until it is the desired consistency. You should not need to add any more salt, but taste just to be sure.

Serve warm with the sauce spooned over, on a bed of polenta, if you'd like to be traditional.

You will find skewers of grilled meats and skinless sausage (*ražniči* and *ćevapčići*) on the menu of many restaurants throughout Balkan countries, and also on the Istrian peninsula. I remember eating them with Ksenija during that summer we spent together in Pola/Pula. Cookbook author Mady Fast believes that they are not Slavic in origin, but of Turkish, Bulgarian or Romani provenance. In our dialect, meat on a skewer is called *carne in speo*, and it is often served with a sauce. I love the simple recipe in Anna Vascotto's book, which this recipe is based on, made with cubes of pork, thickly cut pancetta and fresh sage leaves. As you can see, the dish doesn't need a lot of preparation, cooking or technique. The cooking time in the recipe is for a grill (broiler) or an oven with the upper heating element, but you could also use a barbecue or stovetop grill.

Make sure you use a high-quality cut such as loin, with very little fat; the pancetta adds the fat to the dish. You can easily scale up the quantities. The serve below is for two skewers per person, as part of a meal with a side of potatoes and a salad or vegetable dish, such as Braised peas & fennel (page 165).

Pork & pancetta skewers
(Carne in speo)

Makes 8

400 g (14 oz) pork loin
200 g (7 oz) thickly sliced
  pancetta
24 sage leaves
2 tablespoons extra virgin
  olive oil
sea salt and freshly cracked
  black pepper
a squeeze of lemon juice
  (optional)

Cut the pork and pancetta each into 32 even-sized cubes. Thread metal (or soaked bamboo) skewers with alternating cubes of pork, pancetta and sage leaves.

Place on a baking tray, then drizzle with the extra virgin olive oil and sprinkle over a little salt and pepper.

Preheat a grill (broiler) to medium–high. Place the skewers under the grill for 5 minutes, then turn over and grill the other side for 5 minutes. (You can also place them in a preheated 200°C/400°F fan-forced oven and cook them the same way.)

Serve two skewers per person, with potatoes and a vegetable dish. I enjoy a squeeze of lemon juice on the skewers, as it cuts through the fattiness of the pancetta, but this is purely optional.

SHE PICKED HER FAVOURITE PIECE, A BRACELET WITH EMERALDS

I connected with Tamara through social media. One evening, we caught up to chat about our common heritage. She brought her sister Sandra along, and over a spritz, we got to the all-important questions: where in Istria were her parents born, when did they arrive in Australia, and did they speak *dialetto* (the Istrian–Venetian dialect) at home?

And the connection was real. Their parents were from Torre; Alice, their mother, arrived in Australia in 1950 with her parents and, like me, *dialetto* was the first language they heard. Of even greater coincidence is that the journey of Alice and her family was the same as that of my parents: the same migrant camps in the same year. We are certain they knew each other.

Their father, Erminio, and mother, Alice, had gone to school together in Torre. The years after Istria was ceded to Yugoslavia were difficult ones, and when Erminio was 18, in 1949, he and two friends plotted their escape. In the dead of night, without telling anyone, they took a row boat and rowed along the coast to the Italian border. They were stopped by the Italian *carabinieri* (police) who, as they had no identity papers, threw them in jail. But they were ever so grateful: even though they were in jail, at least they were in Italy. There was no way of sending news back to Torre, so the tiny community, having woken up to empty beds and a missing row boat, assumed the worst.

Erminio was disillusioned with what had happened in post-war Europe, and decided to migrate. He ran into his former school friend Alice at a migrant camp at Cinecittà, near Rome, when starting the process of migration. She could not believe her eyes when she saw him! He was well – and alive – but without a penny (or a *lira*, the Italian currency prior to the Euro) to his name.

She thankfully managed to rustle up a few to give him. Both migrated to Australia separately: Erminio landing in Sydney to work on the Snowy Mountains scheme, and Alice with her parents to Bonegilla, then Melbourne.

In the mid-1950s, Alice took a trip to Sydney to attend a family baptism. There she bumped into Erminio for a second time, near the Trocadero club, where Alice was going dancing with friends. She invited him to join them and they spent a few hours together, reliving memories of Torre and their lives in distant Istria, dancing to the popular tunes of the day. Erminio begged Alice to meet him the next day at a jewellery shop, before she returned to Melbourne. He needed help choosing a gift for a friend. She had little time, but he was so insistent that she finally agreed. In the jewellery store, he asked her to pick her favourite piece. She chose a bracelet with emeralds. 'Are you sure this is your favourite?' he asked. She nodded and waited outside while he paid and had it wrapped. On the street Erminio, presented Alice with the beautifully wrapped box. She was completely taken aback, saying she could not accept the generous gift. Erminio replied that she had to – it was in return for the few *lire* she had given him in 1949 in Cinecittà, when he was destitute. The rest, is, as they say, history.

Erminio and Alice were married and lived in Melbourne, creating an enviable and plentiful vegetable garden. Alice loved to cook, and her traditional dishes brought back memories of Istria, the seasonal ingredients in the garden forming the base for her repertoire of dishes. Tamara shared several of her mother's recipes with me: Alice's tiny meatballs in a rich tomato sauce (page 128) and pan-cooked cabbage with potatoes (page 130), which she made using Erminio's savoy cabbage, with its delightfully corrugated texture.

Scelse il suo gioiello preferito, un
braccialetto con gli smeraldi

My friend Tamara's mother, Alice, gave me this recipe, which is one she remembers making in summer with her mamma. The produce from her father Erminio's garden was collected by the armful: tomatoes, basil, parsley and other fresh herbs. Alice would make a thick, garlicky tomato *sugo* using the tomatoes, and while it was bubbling away on the stove, Tamara would help by rolling the *polpettine*, little meatballs, which would be separately pan-fried and then dropped into the rich, red sauce. A combination of minced (ground) meats was used – two of either beef, veal, pork or chicken – and finely chopped pancetta would be added, too, if there was any in the fridge. Plenty of grated parmesan was scattered on the meatballs at the table.

When I make the recipe I use minced chicken and beef, as I fondly remember my mother combining the two in her *sugo*. It is not a combination you find that often, but it works in this hearty family meal. I have replaced Alice's garden-grown tomatoes with good-quality tinned tomatoes, which are more reliably available through the year.

Alice's meatballs
(Polpettine di Alice)

Makes about 30 meatballs

75 ml (2½ fl oz) extra virgin olive oil
1 brown onion, finely diced
3 garlic cloves, finely diced
900 g (2 lb) tinned whole peeled tomatoes
a few stalks of fresh basil
sea salt
grated parmesan, to serve

For the meatballs

1 slice bread, crust removed
2 tablespoons fresh herb leaves (a mix of parsley and oregano), finely chopped
300 g (10½ oz) minced (ground) beef
300 g (10½ oz) minced (ground) chicken
1 egg

Place 3 tablespoons of the olive oil and the onion in a large frying pan and set over medium heat. Sauté the onion for about 12 minutes; it should be soft, translucent and starting to turn pale golden. Add the garlic and cook for a few minutes until fragrant, then add the tomatoes, including the juice in the tins. Once the sauce starts to bubble, add the basil stalks and reduce the heat. Cover and cook for about 20 minutes, or until the sauce thickens. Season to taste with salt. (Remove the basil stalks before adding the meatballs.)

While the sauce is bubbling away, make the meatballs. Place the bread in a small bowl and add a little water – not too much, just enough that the bread soaks it up and softens. Squeeze the excess water from the bread and place it in a large bowl with the herbs, beef, chicken, egg and ¾ teaspoon of salt. Mix with your hands until well combined. With damp hands, shape into small balls, about the size of a small apricot.

Place the remaining olive oil in a non-stick frying pan over medium heat. Fry the meatballs in batches for 3–4 minutes on each side, until golden brown. Once each batch is browned, I drop them straight into the tomato sauce, to finish cooking. Continue to cook the meatballs in the sauce for another 10 minutes or so. Season to taste with salt.

Serve warm, with plenty of the thick tomato sauce on your plate, a good grating of parmesan and crusty bread.

Potatoes and cabbage were staples of winter meals in Istria; plentiful, filling and affordable. Speck or pancetta add fat and flavour to this simple dish, based on one Alice, my friend Tamara's mother, would make, using savoy cabbage and potatoes from her husband Erminio's garden. I also add sauerkraut for acidity, and caraway seeds for complexity, as I love their fragrant anise-like taste. To make this a complete wintery meal, I like to include a few good-quality pork sausages or partially cured chorizo. Some mustard and a bit of horseradish on the side wouldn't go astray either.

Pan-cooked cabbage with potatoes, speck & sausage
(Verza e patate in tecia)

Serves 6

½ savoy cabbage

sea salt and freshly cracked black pepper

2 large desiree or other all-purpose potatoes, scrubbed, unpeeled

2–3 good-quality pork or chorizo sausages

100 g (3½ oz) speck or pancetta, diced

1 brown onion, diced

3 tablespoons extra virgin olive oil

2 garlic cloves, crushed

250 g (9 oz) sauerkraut, drained

¾ teaspoon caraway seeds, crushed

Roughly chop the cabbage into strips and remove the central spine. Place in a large saucepan of boiling salted water and cook for about 5 minutes. Drain and set aside.

Place the whole potatoes in a saucepan and cover with water. Bring to the boil, season with salt, then reduce the heat and simmer rapidly for 25–30 minutes, until the potatoes are fork-tender, but still whole.

While the potatoes are cooking, pierce the sausages a few times with a fork and place in a small saucepan filled with water. Bring to the boil, then simmer for about 10 minutes, or until cooked through. (You can pan-fry the sausages instead, if you like.) Chop into chunks and set aside.

Place the speck, onion and olive oil in a large heavy-based saucepan over medium–low heat. Sauté for about 25 minutes, stirring occasionally, until the fat renders and the onion has softened, but not browned. Add the garlic and cook until fragrant, then add the cabbage and the drained sauerkraut. Season with salt and pepper to taste.

Stir in the caraway seeds and cook for 5 minutes or so, until all the flavours have combined, then add the sausages. When your potatoes are fork-tender, drain them and drop them whole into the pan. Crush the potatoes with the back of a fork; you want them to be partially mashed, but still have a few chunky pieces. Cook for about 5 minutes, then season to taste with salt.

This dish tastes even better a day or more after it is made – though it is so delicious it probably won't last that long.

Brodetto is a more romantic word for a fish stew, which is typical of the Adriatic coast. It can be made with just one type of fish, or many – often the less prized or uglier ones that fishermen couldn't sell, which they would keep for their own *brodetto*.

This is the version my mother made often, as it was one of my father's favourite dishes, and a simple and relatively quick way to cook firm-fleshed white fish. We usually made it with snapper, buying a whole snapper from the fishmonger and having it cleaned and gutted. As my father would say, how can you trust that the fish is fresh, if you cannot look at its eyes and check they are clear and shiny?

Livia's one-fish stew
(Brodetto de Livia)

Serves 3–4

3 tablespoons extra virgin olive oil
½ large brown onion, finely diced
4–6 oil-preserved anchovy fillets, chopped
1 garlic clove, finely chopped
600 ml (20½ fl oz) good-quality tomato passata (puréed tomatoes)
sea salt
800 g (1 lb 12 oz) snapper (or other firm-fleshed white fish) fillets, skin removed
2 tablespoons plain (all-purpose) flour
1 handful of fresh parsley leaves

Place 2 tablespoons of the olive oil in a large heavy-based frying pan over medium–low heat. Add the onion and anchovy and cook for about 10 minutes, stirring occasionally to ensure that the onion is not catching. The anchovy should dissolve completely, and the onion should be soft and translucent. Add the garlic and cook until fragrant. Next add the passata, rinsing your bottle or tin with 60 ml (¼ cup) of water and stirring that into the sauce as well. Cook for about 30 minutes, until the sauce has thickened. Check for salt before adding the fish.

While the sauce is simmering away, prepare the fish. Cut it into pieces that are about 6 cm x 8 cm (2½ in x 3¼ in) – the exact size will depend on the type of fish you use. Scatter the flour on a large plate and dust both sides of the fish. Place another large frying pan over medium heat and add the remaining oil. Fry the fish – in batches if needed – for a couple of minutes each side; the underside will turn white and then extend towards the middle. When this happens, carefully flip the fish onto the other side. The surface of the fish should be lightly golden, and the centre almost completely cooked.

Carefully slip the fish into the sauce. Cover and simmer for 6–7 minutes, flipping the fish over after 3 minutes.

Scatter plenty of fresh parsley over the top to serve. I love eating this dish with soft polenta, just like we did at home. You can also use bread to mop up the delicious sauce.

I spent several summers at Bibo and Jole's beach house in Blairgowrie (a beachside suburb in Melbourne) during my early teenage years. Jole's father, Toni, was usually at the beach house, too. He was an avid fisherman; back home in Abbazia/Opatija he had owned a fish shop. Every night after dinner he would take his grandson Chris for a walk down the old wooden pier in Blairgowrie to fish for calamari. In the late 1970s, his son-in-law Bibo purchased a speed boat, so in the morning they would head out onto the bay and, after a few hours on the water, they would return home with buckets of freshly caught flathead. Toni would patiently clean and fillet the fish downstairs, then bring it upstairs to Jole for crumbing and frying. We hungry teenagers would wolf down the lot, served with a squeeze of lemon, almost faster than Jole could fry them.

I like to put freshly chopped parsley and pecorino in the crumb, but feel free to substitute the strong-tasting pecorino with parmesan. If you cannot find flathead tails, substitute with other small fish fillets, such as whiting.

Crumbed flathead with pecorino & parsley
(Pesse apanado)

Serves 3–4

50 g (⅓ cup) plain
  (all-purpose) flour
50 g (½ cup) dry breadcrumbs
45 g (½ cup) grated Pecorino
  Romano
1 handful of fresh parsley
  leaves, finely chopped
1 large egg
3 tablespoons milk
750 g (1 lb 11 oz) flathead fillets
2–3 tablespoons extra virgin
  olive oil
sea salt flakes, for sprinkling
lemon wedges, to serve

Prepare two plates and a shallow bowl – place the flour on one plate; mix the breadcrumbs, cheese and parsley on the other plate; and lightly whisk the egg and milk in the bowl.

Wash your fish fillets and pat dry. Place the fillets one at a time in the flour, then the egg wash, then the crumb mixture, making sure they are well coated in each before moving to the next. Place the crumbed fish fillets on a plate.

Place the oil in a large non-stick frying pan over medium heat. Pan-fry the fish in batches, carefully wiping the pan with paper towel if there are any burnt crumbs remaining after each batch, and adding a splash more oil if needed. The cooking time will depend on how thick the fish fillets are, but usually 3–4 minutes on one side and 2 minutes on the other side is just right. The crumb should be golden and the fish cooked through.

Scatter with salt flakes and serve hot, with lemon wedges.

In the north-east corner of Italy, from Chioggia just south of Venice, up to Trieste, and then all along the Istrian and Dalmatian coast, you will find various types of seafood dishes *alla busara* – often scampi or prawns (shrimp) cooked in a sauce of tomatoes, parsley and garlic.

The word *busara* is generally thought to derive from the pan used by sailors on a boat to cook fish, but Francesco Gottardi believes that the word *busa* (which means 'hole' in the Istrian–Venetian dialect) comes from cooking in a *busa* – a hole in the ground, not a pan on a boat. Gottardi writes that after large pieces of meat were cooked in the busa, the remaining heat was used to cook other foods at low temperature. His recipe has sardine fillets layered with thinly sliced potatoes, smothered in garlic, parsley and olive oil, cooked slowly in the oven and then finished on the stove. The result is deliciously tender sardine fillets, with plenty of garlic-infused olive oil, lovely for dunking bread at the end of the meal. And not a tomato in sight.

Slow-cooked sardines
(Busara de sarde)

Serves 3–4 as a light meal

300 g (10½ oz) potatoes, scrubbed, unpeeled

1 handful of parsley leaves, finely chopped, plus extra chopped parsley to serve

1 large garlic clove, finely chopped

sea salt and freshly cracked black pepper

500 g (1 lb 2 oz) sardine fillets, butterflied

3–4 tablespoons extra virgin olive oil

You will need a flameproof casserole dish that will fit all the sardines and potatoes in several layers. Mine measured 24 cm (9½ in) in diameter.

Place the potatoes in a saucepan of cold salted water and bring to the boil. Cook for 12–17 minutes, until they are just cooked through. Do not overcook. Drain, then peel the potatoes and cut them into 3–4 mm (⅛–¼ in) thick slices.

Combine the parsley and garlic in a small bowl and season with salt and pepper.

Preheat the oven to 80°C (175°F) fan-forced.

Wash the sardines and pat dry. Add just enough olive oil to your pan to cover the base. Scatter in some of the parsley and garlic, then add a layer of sardines, skin side down. Next, add all the potato slices, in a single layer. Scatter over more parsley and garlic, a tiny bit of the remaining oil, then another layer of sardines, this time skin side up. Top with more parsley, garlic and a bit more olive oil (not too much).

Cover the pan with a tight-fitting lid, then roast for 20 minutes.

Remove the pan from the oven. Keeping the lid on, place the pan on the stovetop over medium heat for 5–7 minutes, until the oil is bubbling and the sardines are cooked. Remove from the heat, leave covered and allow to rest for a few minutes.

Enjoy warm or at room temperature. Scatter with extra parsley and serve with a glass of Malvasia or other crisp white wine.

When someone in the family was feeling unwell, especially with a tummy upset, Mamma would make us fish, chicken or meat *in bianco*. This literally translates to 'dressed in white', meaning the meat was steamed or poached, then served with a light dressing of olive oil and/or lemon juice. Although I was not a fan of poached meat or chicken, I love steamed fish, especially when you dress it up just a bit.

I found a terrific recipe for a sauce to have with steamed fish in Mady Fast's book on Istrian cooking, attributed to Iolanda Madieri from Fiume/Rijeka. The sauce is a lovely balance of savoury, eggy and vinegary, to which I have added just a bit of sweetness. It may not fit in with Mamma's definition of *in bianco*, but I think she may have approved. You can make the sauce a day or two earlier and store it in a sealed jar in the fridge. It becomes milder and more delicious over time.

Here I've used red snapper fillets, but feel free to use any firm-fleshed white fish fillets.

Steamed snapper with Iolanda's sauce
(Pese con la salsa de Iolanda)

Serves 6

1.2 kg (2 lb 10 oz) firm-fleshed
   white fish fillets, such as
   snapper or hapuka
extra virgin olive oil, for
   drizzling

For the sauce

2 eggs, at room temperature
1 slice bread, crust removed
2 tablespoons white wine
   vinegar
2 spring onions (scallions)
1 heaped tablespoon parsley
   leaves, plus extra to serve
100 ml (3½ fl oz) extra virgin
   olive oil
pinch of sugar, to taste
sea salt and freshly cracked
   black pepper

Start by making the sauce. Place the eggs in a small saucepan and cover with water. Bring to the boil, then cover and remove from the heat. Allow the eggs to sit in the water for 10 minutes, to hard-boil them. Drain and allow to cool slightly before peeling and roughly chopping the eggs.

While the eggs are cooking, tear the bread into rough pieces and place in a small bowl. Pour the vinegar over and allow to soak for a few minutes.

Chop the white parts of the spring onions and place in a mini food processor. Chop the green parts and reserve for garnishing.

Add the eggs to the food processor, along with the bread (don't drain it – it should have absorbed all the vinegar) and parsley. Blend roughly; the mixture will be quite dry at this stage. Add 80 ml (⅓ cup) of the olive oil and pulse until a thick sauce forms. If needed, add a little more of the oil – up to 1 tablespoon – to get the consistency to your liking. Add the sugar and salt and pepper to taste, then give it another pulse. Spoon into a small serving dish, garnish with the reserved spring onion and extra chopped parsley, and set aside while you steam the fish.

Pour 5 cm (2 in) of water into the bottom of your steamer (I improvise a steamer using a metal colander in a large saucepan). Bring to the boil and place the fish fillets in the steamer rack (or colander) and place in the pan. The base of the rack (or colander) should be above the water line, as you want the fish to cook via steam, not boil in the water.

Cover and reduce the heat so that the water simmers and continues to produce steam. The actual cooking time depends on the size of your fish fillets – anywhere between 4 and 10 minutes. The flesh should have turned completely white when you pierce the inner part, and easily flake with a fork.

Carefully remove the cooked fillets from the steamer and place on your serving plate. Drizzle with the remaining olive oil, garnish with extra parsley, sprinkle with sea salt, and pass the sauce around to spoon on top.

My distant cousin Tara, who lives near Cittanova/Novigrad, sent me a photo on Instagram. It simply said, 'Today for lunch we had cuttlefish.' When I questioned her further (as Istrian seafood is second to none), she told me it was a recipe that her great-grandmother Angelina from Cittanova used to make. Cittanova is a pretty fishing village, with colourful houses and a 16th-century arched Venetian loggia right on the water. The secret ingredient, she wrote – and I was surprised to read – was cinnamon.

I have added peas to make it more of a complete dish (plus I love the green!), and omitted the ink of the cuttlefish, but otherwise it is true to Angelina's recipe. A warning about the cinnamon: you only need a little bit. It gives the dish a lovely warmth, a sweetness that balances the freshness of the peas and parsley. Tara serves the cuttlefish with plain rice, but I love the dish with polenta.

Angelina's braised cuttlefish with peas & cinnamon
(Seppie e piselli di Angelina) ·

Serves 2–3 as a main

4 medium to large cuttlefish, about 900 g (2 lb) before cleaning, and 450 g (1 lb) after cleaning

3 tablespoons extra virgin olive oil

1 small brown onion, grated or finely chopped

sea salt and freshly cracked black pepper

1 large garlic clove, finely diced

a good handful of parsley leaves, finely chopped

80 ml (⅓ cup) dry white wine

155 g (1 cup) frozen peas

¼ teaspoon ground cinnamon

polenta (see page 247), to serve

Wash and clean the cuttlefish (or ask your fishmonger to do this for you), retaining the hood and tentacles. Score the inner flesh in a crisscross pattern, then chop into bite-sized pieces. Roughly chop the tentacles. Set aside.

Place the olive oil and onion in a large frying pan over medium–low heat. Add a pinch of salt and cook for about 10 minutes. Add the garlic and fry for a few minutes, until fragrant.

Increase the heat to medium and add the cuttlefish and half the parsley. Once it has warmed through, increase the heat, then add the wine and allow it to mostly evaporate. Reduce the heat to medium, pour in 60 ml (¼ cup) of hot water and cover the pan. Simmer for about 25 minutes.

Add the peas, then cover and continue to simmer for another 10 minutes. If there is too much liquid, remove the lid and increase the heat for a few minutes until it is reduced. Add the cinnamon and season with salt and pepper, then scatter over the remaining parsley.

Serve on warmed plates, with polenta, potatoes, rice or crusty bread to mop up the sauce.

Vegetables

Verdure

Potatoes and silverbeet are a frequent accompaniment to oven-baked or grilled fish and other seafood dishes in Istrian and Dalmatian cooking; at home we called the dish *patate e blede*. I loved nothing better than to top it with my mamma's meat *sugo* or a simple tomato salsa; this memory is my inspiration for the recipe below.

It is a more substantial version, with potatoes and silverbeet layered in a baking dish, with eggs, milk and cheese to bind it all together. I like to top it with roasted cherry tomatoes, visually more appealing than spooning on a red sauce. It is simple, delicious and hearty – vegetarian comfort food at its best. Eat it piping hot from the oven, or at room temperature.

Silverbeet & potato bake with roasted cherry tomatoes
(Sformato di blede e patate con pomodorini)

Serves 2, or 4 as a side dish

250 g (9 oz) potatoes (old floury
    ones are best)
sea salt and freshly cracked
    black pepper
250 g (9 oz) silverbeet
    (Swiss chard)
60 ml (¼ cup) extra virgin olive
    oil, plus extra for drizzling
1 garlic clove, finely chopped
vine-ripened cherry tomatoes
    (as many as you like)
4 tablespoons dry breadcrumbs,
    preferably homemade
4 eggs
250 ml (1 cup) milk
50 g (½ cup) grated parmesan
40 g (1½ oz) mild semi-matured
    cow's milk cheese (I use Piave),
    thinly sliced

Peel the potatoes and cut into 5 cm (2 in) dice. Place in a saucepan of cold water, bring to the boil and add a good pinch of salt. Cook for about 10 minutes, or until cooked through but still whole. Drain and set aside to cool.

Meanwhile, wash and drain the silverbeet. Trim the stalks, keeping 5 cm (2 in) attached to the leaf. Chop into 3 cm (1¼ in) pieces.

Preheat the oven to 180°C (350°F) fan-forced.

Place a large frying pan over medium heat. Add 1 tablespoon of the olive oil and sauté the garlic until fragrant. Add the silverbeet leaves and stalks and fry for about 5 minutes, or until the stalks have softened, and everything is infused with garlic. Set aside.

Place the cherry tomatoes in a baking dish, drizzle with 1 tablespoon of the olive oil (or a bit more if needed) and place in the oven. They will probably need about 10 minutes more baking time than the main dish, but it does depend on the size of your tomatoes, so keep checking on them. The tomatoes are ready when they have split slightly and are starting to brown.

To assemble the bake – drizzle the remaining oil over the base of a baking dish (mine measured 20 cm x 25 cm/8 in x 10 in) and smear it up the sides. Scatter half the breadcrumbs around the dish. Layer the silverbeet and potato in the dish.

In a bowl, whisk the eggs and milk with a fork to combine. Stir in most of the parmesan and season with salt and pepper. Pour the mixture over the vegetables. Arrange the cheese slices over the top and scatter with the remaining parmesan. Drizzle with olive oil, then scatter with the remaining breadcrumbs.

Bake for 20 minutes, or until the bake is golden on top and the egg has cooked through.

Leave to cool slightly, then cut into squares. Top with the roasted tomatoes and serve.

The bake keeps for a few days in an airtight container in the fridge. You can serve it at room temperature or reheat. The roasted tomatoes are best eaten on the day they are made.

In his book about the food of Fiume/Rijeka, Francesco Gottardi dedicates an entire chapter to goulash (*gulyas*, as he calls it). Goulash is traditionally a soupy beef stew, flavoured with paprika, and Hungarian in origin. The Austro–Hungarian empire stretched across large parts of Europe in the 1700s and 1800s, with many towns adopting their own variations of this hearty dish. In Austria, cumin and marjoram were added; along the north-eastern coast of Italy, small quantities of tomato were added; and then in more recent times, red capsicum (bell pepper) was added. Gottardi describes goulash variants, including a rather delicious vegetarian one made with mushrooms and red capsicum. He adds a generous amount of cream, to make a silky and deliciously smoky stew, though I often leave it out, so my vegan friends can enjoy the dish.

Mushroom & capsicum goulash
(Gulash di funghi e peperoni)

Serves 4, or 8 as a side dish

15 g (½ oz) dried porcini mushrooms

1 kg (2 lb 3 oz) field, flat or Swiss Brown mushrooms (or a mix)

80 ml (⅓ cup) extra virgin olive oil

1 large brown onion, finely diced

sea salt

2 garlic cloves, thinly sliced

2 red capsicums (bell peppers), cut into thin strips

125 ml (½ cup) dry white wine

125 ml (½ cup) tomato passata (puréed tomatoes)

1½ teaspoons sweet paprika

½ scant teaspoon smoked hot paprika

1 teaspoon ground cumin

½ teaspoon dried thyme

2 tablespoons good-quality red wine vinegar

200 ml (7 fl oz) pouring (single/light) cream (optional)

fresh thyme or parsley leaves, to serve

Soak the dried mushrooms in about 150 ml (5 fl oz) hot (not boiling) water for at least 15 minutes, to soften them. Drain, reserving the liquid, and chop the rehydrated mushrooms into bite-sized pieces. Set aside.

Trim the mushroom stalks, then wipe the tops clean with a clean tea towel. Cut into slices about 7–8 mm (⅓ in) thick. Set aside.

Place the olive oil in a large flameproof casserole dish over medium heat. Add the onion with a pinch of salt and cook for about 10 minutes, stirring occasionally, so the onion does not take on too much colour. Add the garlic and cook until fragrant, then add the fresh mushroom, rehydrated porcini and the capsicum. Allow to warm through, stirring occasionally.

Increase the heat and add the wine. Allow the wine to evaporate a little, then reduce the heat and stir in the passata. Mix the spices and thyme into the reserved porcini stock (warm it up if it has cooled down) until well combined, then add that too. Season with salt to taste.

Cover and cook over medium–low heat for 10 minutes. Remove the lid and cook for another 10 minutes, or until the vegetables have cooked through, stirring occasionally. If serving this as a vegan dish, then don't let all of the liquid evaporate, to retain some of the sauciness. If adding cream, cook until most of the liquid has evaporated. Stir in the vinegar and season to taste with salt.

Add the cream (if using) just before serving, stirring so it is evenly mixed through the vegetables.

Scatter over some fresh thyme or parsley and serve warm, with polenta or mashed potatoes.

Iolanda de Vonderweid describes an old recipe from Albona/Labin for a simple potato and mushroom bake that she calls a *tortino*. Layers of sliced potatoes alternate with sliced mushrooms, with plenty of garlic, parsley and olive oil in between. I slice the potatoes very thinly, with a mandoline, as thinly as a pasta sheet. Although the original recipe calls for fresh porcini mushrooms, a combination of large tasty field or flat mushrooms and dried porcini makes a fine substitute for the meaty fresh porcini. The addition of a layer of sliced red onion adds a hint of sweetness, and a drizzle of aged balsamic vinegar just before serving takes this humble dish, which looks a bit like a tray of pasta-free lasagne, to another level. I like adding a semi-matured mild cow's milk cheese, such as Montasio, Piave or Asiago, on the second layer of potatoes, as it binds it together better (and makes it taste even more delicious). You could also use a mild cheddar.

Mushroom, potato & onion bake
(Tortino di funghi e patate)

Serves 3–4

15 g (½ oz) dried porcini
  mushrooms
olive oil, for drizzling
500 g (1 lb 2 oz) large potatoes,
  very thinly sliced
sea salt and freshly cracked
  black pepper
1 small red onion, very thinly
  sliced
500 g (1 lb 2 oz) field
  mushrooms, thickly sliced,
  about 10–12 mm (½ in) thick
1 handful of parsley leaves,
  finely chopped, plus extra
  to serve
2 large garlic cloves, finely
  chopped
60 g (2 oz) mild semi-matured
  cow's milk cheese, thinly sliced
80 g (2¾ oz) parmesan, shaved
aged balsamic vinegar, to serve
  (optional)

Soak the dried mushrooms in 60 ml (¼ cup) hot (not boiling) water for at least 15 minutes. Drain, reserving the liquid, and chop the rehydrated mushrooms into small pieces. Set aside.

Preheat the oven to 180°C (350°F) fan-forced.

Drizzle some of the olive oil around a baking dish; mine measured 24 cm x 32 cm (9½ in x 12¾ in). Place one-third of the potato slices in the dish in a slightly overlapping layer, along with a sprinkling of salt and pepper. Add half the onion and half the fresh mushrooms, another sprinkling of salt and pepper, and half the porcini. Scatter over half the parsley and garlic, then half the semi-matured cheese. Drizzle with a little more olive oil, and half the reserved porcini stock.

Add another layer of potato; sprinkle with salt and pepper. On top, layer the remaining semi-matured cheese, onion, fresh mushrooms, porcini, parsley and garlic. Season again with salt and pepper. Drizzle over a bit more olive oil and the remaining porcini stock. Add the final layer of potato. Drizzle with more olive oil and arrange the shaved parmesan on top.

Cover with foil and bake for 45 minutes. Remove the foil and bake for another 15 minutes, or until the top is golden and you are sure the potatoes are cooked through. Allow to cool (covered with the foil) for 15 minutes.

Serve garnished with extra parsley, with a drizzle of balsamic vinegar, if desired.

YOU KNOW I LOVE YOU AND THAT YOU ARE EVERYTHING TO ME

The Carli family moved to Monfalcone in the late 1930s. They ran bars, and the move made good business sense. Monfalcone was a busy hub and the site of a major ship-building yard, so there were jobs for the two Carli boys, and the three Carli girls would work in the family bars.

In 1947 the region of Venezia Giulia was split into four broad areas that centred around the so-called Morgan Line, between Italy and Yugoslavia, with a relatively neutral zone in between. Along that line, Monfalcone was the first major town in Italy, and my father, Nello, and his family were among the *profughi Istriani* (Istrian refugees) to settle there. The influx of many thousands of Istrians was met with some anger by the locals, as jobs and accommodation in the initial post-war period were scarce and seemed to be given preferentially to them. My *nonna* feared that her two youngest unmarried daughters would meet *profughi* rather than hard-working local boys. Even though they were all from the region of Venezia Giulia, the Istrians were considered a little wilder and less predictable than the *Monfalconesi*, prone to having itchy feet and a desire to travel.

Much to my *nonna's* dismay, the Istrian Assistance office was over the road from the bar they owned, *'Bar alla Posta'*. It was good for business, but she worried for her two daughters, Clara and Livia. When Matteo Bacchia and his son Nello stopped at the bar for a coffee, they made quite an impression. Both were tall and polite, with broad smiles. Nello, with his piercing blue eyes and smooth voice, wasted no time in charming 19-year old Livia, who worked front-of-house. He wanted to ask her out, but she didn't get much time off, and her sister Clara would need to be chaperone.

And her ever-present father, Francesco, also suspicious of *istriani*, made it more difficult to even chat to her.

The story goes that one day Livia had hurt her hand and her mother had given her the afternoon off work. Wearing her best clothes, she went to the Cinema Azzurro, to see her favourite actor, Gregory Peck, in his latest (badly dubbed) Hollywood movie. Nello happened to see her leave home, which was above the bar, and followed her, at a good distance, to see where she was going. He followed her into the cinema, and once the movie started, without her noticing, sat close to her. She was so involved with Gregory Peck and his lady on the screen that she failed to see that Nello was now sitting beside her. He leant across and planted a kiss on her cheek. She looked at him in horror, and ran out of the cinema, down the Corso, across the piazza, down Via Sant'Ambrogio and into her home to wash her face.

Once she recovered from the shock, Livia started thinking about this striking *istriano*, who was possibly more handsome than Gregory Peck. Their subsequent meetings were less dramatic; a friendship developed, and that turned into something more. Nello's family moved to Varese, close to Milano, as his father, Matteo, had secured a job at the post office there – so Nello travelled between the two cities to spend time with his sweetheart. He wrote Livia a letter from Varese in December 1947, asking if the tears she had shed when he was boarding the train in Monfalcone had dried, because they were not needed. The letter ends with '*Tu lo sai che ti voglio tanto bene, e sei tutto per me*' ('You know I love you and that you are everything to me').

My parents married one Monday morning in August 1948. Nello had a job in the local ship-building yard and my *nonna* was happy. It seemed that her youngest daughter, the sunny-natured, hard-working Livia, would remain in Monfalcone, even though she had married an Istrian rather than a local boy. What my *nonna* didn't yet know was that in 1950 Livia and her son-in-law would leave Italy on the ship *General Greeley*. Australia had opened up its borders for European migrants displaced by war as part of an assisted passage scheme; they would have free travel by ship, in exchange for two years of work in whatever jobs the government gave them. Nello qualified for the scheme, as his homeland had been upended by war, and desiring to see the world, he jumped at the opportunity, taking his new and somewhat reluctant bride with him.

Tu lo sai che
ti voglio tanto bene,
e sei tutto per me

When my mother arrived in Australia aged 22, she couldn't really cook. She had worked front-of-house in her parents' bars, but they always had a cook. Having an Istrian husband, who lived for good food, proved to be somewhat of a challenge. He was not adventurous in the kitchen; a whiff of something that was foreign to him and he wouldn't even try it. He craved dishes that reminded him of home. Luckily they had a network of friends who were mainly from Istria, and my mother learned to cook from these Istrian ladies: Gemma, Jolanda, Maria, Alba and Emma. She perfected a handful of dishes that made my father very happy, and one of them was this – *patate in tecia*, which literally means 'potatoes in the pan'. Cooked potatoes are roughly smashed into onion that has been cooked slowly in plenty of olive oil. It is a bit like a vegan version of mashed potatoes. Don't be alarmed by the amount of olive oil that is used, as olive oil is extremely good for you. It is a deceptively simple dish, but very, very good.

Smashed potatoes with onion & olive oil
(Patate in tecia)

Serves 4 as a side dish

750 g (1 lb 11 oz) mashing potatoes (such as king william, desiree, Dutch cream)

sea salt

1 large onion, about 280 g (10 oz)

80 ml (⅓ cup) good-quality extra virgin olive oil

Wash and peel the potatoes, then cut into large chunks. Place them in a saucepan and cover with plenty of cold water. Bring to the boil slowly, add a good pinch of salt, then cook for 10–15 minutes, until the potato is fork-tender but still whole. The cooking time will depend on the size of the potatoes.

While the potato is cooking, cut the onion into 2–3 mm (⅛–⅙ in) thick rings, then cut the rings in half, into semi-circles. Pour the olive oil into a saucepan large enough to fit the potato; it should thickly cover the base. Add the onion with a pinch of salt and cook over medium–low heat for about 25 minutes, or until the onion is lightly caramelised and pale golden.

Drain the potato well, reserving a little of the cooking water in case the potato becomes too dry. Stir the potato through the caramelised onion, mashing roughly with a fork; the potato should start breaking apart. You don't want a smooth purée – having the occasional small potato chunk is part of the charm of this dish. Add some of the reserved potato cooking water if it looks a bit dry, stirring well, until you are happy with the consistency. Season with salt to taste.

Remove from the heat and serve immediately.

I have a memory prior to school age and it has to do with artichokes. I am in the kitchen, watching my mother clear the dinner table of glasses, cutlery, napkins and plates piled high with remnants of artichoke leaves. This was before I ate artichokes, when I would be fed a bowl of soup or pasta while the adults ate grown-up dishes. The leaves had odd-shaped marks in them, representing the imprints of teeth: the flesh was removed from each artichoke leaf by pulling it out of the mouth through clenched teeth, capturing the deliciousness of each leaf. I felt very grown-up when I was shown how to eat an artichoke. It was not, however, love at first sight. The taste is ever so slightly bitter, getting sweeter the closer the leaf is to the heart. As I grew, so did my love for these wonderful flowers – and when they are in season, I like nothing better than to make them exactly the way my mother did. As written by Mady Fast, '*L'articioco peverin vol oieto e sai vin*' ('Artichokes are best eaten with a good olive oil and a lot of wine'). Luckily this dish uses both.

Livia's stuffed artichokes
(Carciofi ripieni alla Livia)

Serves 4 as a starter

1 large lemon
4 large globe artichokes
2 garlic cloves, finely chopped
1 handful of parsley leaves,
	finely chopped
3 eggs, lightly beaten
100 g (1 cup) grated parmesan,
	plus extra if needed
sea salt and freshly cracked
	black pepper
2 tablespoons olive oil
250 ml (1 cup) dry white wine

Cut the lemon in half. Squeeze the juice into a large bowl of water, and reserve the lemon halves.

Working with one artichoke at a time, cut off and reserve the stem at the base of the flower. Check that you have cut the base of each artichoke so that it is level with the flower and stands upright. Rub the base of the flower with a lemon half to stop it turning brown. Reserve the upper 5 cm (2 in) of stem, and discard the lower part. Trim the thick outer green part of the stem with a sharp knife, then place the central trimmed stem in the bowl of acidulated water.

Next, work on the artichoke flower. Cut off the top quarter of the flower, remove the outer leaves from the base (one or two layers, depending on the artichoke). Using scissors, trim any spiky tops from the next layer of leaves. Prise open the central portion of the artichoke, removing any hard central leaves that prevent you accessing the centre. If there is a hairy choke, remove it using a small teaspoon. Place the trimmed artichoke in the acidulated water, then start on the next one.

To make the stuffing, place the garlic, parsley, egg and parmesan in a bowl and mix until well combined. The mixture should be quite thick; add more parmesan if needed. Season with salt and pepper.

Drain the artichokes and place them upside down for a few minutes, to drain all the water from them. Spoon some filling into the centre of an artichoke where the choke previously was, and between the leaves that are close to the centre. Spoon some filling on top of the artichoke too. Repeat with the remaining filling and artichokes.

Pour the olive oil into a saucepan that is large enough to hold all four artichokes upright. Place the artichokes upright in the saucepan, as well as the trimmed stems. Carefully pour in the wine, and enough water to reach nearly halfway up the artichokes.

Cover and bring to the boil, then reduce the heat and simmer for at least 45 minutes to 1 hour, depending on the size of your artichokes, as well as their age. Older ones can take a little longer to cook.

The artichokes are cooked when a fork easily pierces them. If there is still a lot of water in the pan, remove the artichokes and stems and put the heat on high to evaporate the liquid, so that only a bit of the sauce is left. Spoon the sauce over the cooked artichokes and serve warm.

My father used to grow zucchini in the backyard, mainly to please my mother, as he thought they were a nuisance, long trails seeming to grow overnight to overtake the brick path between rows of vegetables. Mamma used to grate them into her meatballs, and crumb them before frying or grilling them. She occasionally braised them with lots of garlic, white wine and parsley, sometimes throwing in some ham to make him happy, as he was of the general opinion that zucchini were not only a waste of garden space, but tasteless.

I came across a recipe for *Zuchete in tecia* (braised baby zucchini), which Iolanda de Vonderweid and Lidia Bastianich both refer to as an ancient recipe, where cinnamon is added to thinly sliced zucchini rounds. It sounded interesting, but I wanted to add some complexity, so taking inspiration from my mother, I added garlic, anchovies and white wine for depth of flavour, stirring a few teaspoons of white wine vinegar through at the end for balance. Really, there is only a dash of cinnamon, but it adds a hint of dusty sweetness, and makes a tasty dish out of what is not, according to some, a very interesting vegetable. It is a great side dish to grilled or roasted fish.

Braised zucchini with cinnamon
(Zuchete in tecia con cannella)

Serves 6–8 as a side dish

1 kg (2 lb 3 oz) zucchini
  (courgettes)
2–3 tablespoons extra virgin
  olive oil
1 garlic clove, sliced
4 oil-preserved anchovy fillets,
  chopped
1 handful of parsley leaves,
  chopped
60 ml (¼ cup) white wine
1 scant tablespoon white wine
  vinegar
⅛ teaspoon ground cinnamon
sea salt

Cut the zucchini into thin rounds using a mandoline.

Place the oil in a large saucepan over low heat. Add the garlic, anchovy and half the parsley. Cook for a few minutes, until the anchovy dissolves and the garlic is fragrant. Add the zucchini and sauté for a few minutes, until warmed through.

Turn up the heat and add the wine. Allow it to evaporate for a few minutes, then reduce the heat, cover and cook for 10 minutes, until the zucchini rounds soften. Check on them every few minutes and stir, so that they don't catch on the base of the pan. Remove the lid and cook for a further 10 minutes, so the liquid in the base of the pan can reduce.

When the zucchini has cooked through and the liquid has evaporated, remove from the heat and stir through the vinegar, along with the cinnamon and remaining parsley. Add salt to taste.

Serve warm or at room temperature.

Usually I cook peas in the pan for no more than 10 minutes, as I love their slightly firm texture. Mamma would cook them to the point where they could be mashed with the slightest pressure from a fork. This dish, based on one by Anna Vascotto, marries peas with fennel, to make a wonderful sweet braise. I love adding a few handfuls of fresh herbs to the vegetables just before serving, and lemon zest for a lovely citrus balance. Enjoy as a side dish to grilled meats; it goes well with the pork skewers on page 125. It can also easily become the base of a risotto or a pasta sauce. To me, it just tastes like home, even if I keep the peas on the firmer side.

Braised peas & fennel
(Finoci e bisi in tecia)

Serves 6 as a side dish

1 small brown onion
1 small fennel bulb, about
    400 g (14 oz)
3 tablespoons extra virgin
    olive oil
sea salt and freshly cracked
    black pepper
60 ml (¼ cup) dry white wine
60 ml (¼ cup) Really good
    vegetable stock (page 244)
350 g (2⅓ cups) baby peas
    (fresh or frozen)
1 handful of fresh herbs, such
    as parsley and/or dill, chopped,
    to serve
lemon zest, to taste

Slice the onion into fairly thin wedges. Cut the fennel bulb into quarters, and each of the quarters into four or five wedges.

Place the olive oil in a large frying pan over medium–low heat. Add the onion and a pinch of salt and cook for about 8 minutes, until softened, stirring occasionally so it does not stick or brown.

Increase the heat and add the fennel and wine. Once most of the wine has evaporated, add the stock. When the stock comes to the boil, reduce the heat, cover and simmer for about 10 minutes, until the fennel is tender. It should be cooked through, but still have some resistance.

Add the peas and continue to simmer, uncovered, over medium–low heat for about 10 minutes, or until the peas are cooked to your liking. Season with salt and pepper to taste. There should not be much liquid left in the pan, but if there is, increase the heat for a few minutes until it evaporates.

Serve scattered with the fresh herbs and lemon zest.

Istrians love their potatoes. They don't take much effort to grow – once the roots form from old potatoes in the pantry, place them root-side down in the soil – and they store well in a dark, cool place. We ate this simple dish at home all the time, made with new-season potatoes, which keep their shape when cooked. The version I grew up with had just green beans (*fasoleti*), potatoes and a dressing of wine vinegar and olive oil. My father liked slices of home-grown raw garlic with the dish, which added a real kick (and a strong smell, too!). Maybe this was the secret to him living to 90 years of age. I don't add sliced garlic, but love rubbing it on the inner surface of the serving bowl, to impart a subtle garlic flavour. I also add thinly sliced red onion and green olives. Feel free to add other ingredients, such as thinly sliced capsicum (bell pepper) or radishes and different fresh herbs.

Salad dressings are a very personal thing. I make mine in a glass jar, starting with excellent-quality olive oil, and adding vinegar to taste. I use white wine or red wine vinegar and balance out the acidity with a bit of sugar, or use a ready-made white or dark balsamic dressing (which is slightly sweet) with the wine vinegar. I use the general ratio of two-thirds olive oil to one-third vinegar; occasionally I add half a teaspoon of French mustard, too. Then I give the jar a good shake before pouring the dressing on my salad.

Potato & green bean salad
(Patate e fasoleti in insalata)

Serves 6 as a filling side dish

3 waxy potatoes (nicola and
    desiree work well), about
    750 g (1 lb 10½ oz)
sea salt
300 g (11 oz) green beans
iced water
2 tablespoons excellent-quality
    extra virgin olive oil
1 tablespoon white wine vinegar
1 teaspoon white balsamic
    dressing or a pinch of caster
    (superfine) sugar
1 garlic clove, peeled
¼ red onion, thinly sliced
1 handful of crushed green
    pitted olives
1 tablespoon chopped parsley
sea salt flakes

Scrub the potatoes, then place in a saucepan of cold water and set over medium heat. Bring to the boil, season with salt, then simmer for 20–25 minutes, until fork-tender. Drain, then peel while still hot and cut into bite-sized pieces.

While the potatoes are cooking, top and tail the beans, then cut any larger ones in half. Bring a small saucepan of salted water to the boil and drop in the beans. Simmer for 2–5 minutes, depending on how soft you like them. Drain the beans, then place in a bowl of iced water to keep them bright green and stop them cooking further. Allow to cool completely.

To make a salad dressing, place the olive oil, vinegar and white balsamic dressing or sugar in a jar. Seal the jar and shake until well combined.

Rub the garlic around the inner surface of your salad bowl. Discard the garlic, or save for another use. Place the cooled potato in the bowl and gently toss the salad dressing through. (I like to dress the potato at this stage, so the dressing coats it evenly, and the garlic flavour is picked up from the bowl.)

Add the beans, onion, olives and parsley and mix using your hands, rather than salad servers, which might break up the potato. Add sea salt flakes to taste.

You can allow the salad to sit, covered, for several hours before serving.

A recipe book about the memories of my *istriani* friends and family would not be complete without recipes for *fasoi* (beans), an essential ingredient in their kitchens. Borlotti beans in particular were a staple in my father's garden; every year he would plant two rows of them along one of the large garden beds. He would coax the spindly green stalks to wind up around the stakes, tying them at intervals until they were almost as tall as he was. When it was time to harvest them, we would all help, collecting the browning pods from the stalks and then shelling the lot at the kitchen table.

When the beans were fresh, Mamma would cook them in a pot of water with a few other vegetables, until they were just tender. They maintained their shape and had just a bit of bite. A bowl of borlotti beans cooked in this way was kept in the fridge for a few days, and handfuls of beans were added to salads – usually with *radiceto* (leafy green chicory/endive) and thinly sliced onion, doused in extra virgin olive oil and red wine vinegar. This is not really a recipe – more a way of cooking the fresh beans.

Fresh borlotti beans in a salad
(Fasoi in insalata)

Makes enough for 3 salads

600 g (1 lb 5 oz) fresh borlotti (cranberry) beans
½ carrot, chopped
½ celery stalk, chopped
½ small brown onion, chopped in half
1 bay leaf
a few whole black peppercorns
sea salt

Pod the beans, discarding the shells. Place the beans, carrot, celery, onion, bay leaf and peppercorns in a saucepan. Pour in enough water to cover the ingredients by at least 5 cm (2 in).

Bring to the boil, add salt to the water, then reduce the heat to a low, steady boil. Cook for about 20 minutes, until the beans are cooked through, but still retain their shape. Drain the beans and cool under a running tap to stop them cooking. Set aside to drain and cool.

Serve the beans in a salad with good-quality olive oil and your favourite vinegar – either on their own, or with radicchio, thinly sliced onion or your favourite salad ingredients.

You can also eat the other cooked vegetables, which are nicer while they are still warm (or you could feed them to your worm farm!).

Cakes & desserts

Dolci

I have always loved this cake – the sweet ricotta dotted with grappa-soaked sultanas and pine nuts, with a hint of citrus throughout. I still make it in Mamma's old metal cake tin with its rounded edges. Every time I bake it, I think of our times together in the kitchen. If she let me stir the ricotta filling I would sneak quite a few spoonfuls before she spread it over the base, prompting her to comment that there was always less than she thought she had prepared.

This cake tastes much better when it has cooled completely, and even better the next day, perhaps for breakfast with a cup of espresso. Some who have made this cake have substituted the sultanas for chocolate chips, which, if you love chocolate, would also work well.

Livia's ricotta cake
(Dolce di ricotta di Livia)

Serves 16

For the filling

500 g (2 cups) ricotta, drained
40 g (1½ oz) self-raising flour
1 egg
2 tablespoons sultanas (golden raisins), soaked in grappa for at least 2 hours, drained
80 g (⅓ cup) caster sugar
zest of ½ lemon
zest of ½ orange
2 tablespoons pine nuts, toasted

For the batter

2 large eggs, lightly beaten
100 g (3½ oz) unsalted butter, melted then cooled, plus extra for greasing
100 g (3½ oz) caster sugar
zest ½ lemon
250 g (1⅔ cups) self-raising flour
185 ml (¾ cup) milk, plus extra if needed
1 teaspoon pure vanilla extract
pinch of salt

Preheat the oven to 150°C (300°F) fan-forced. Butter the base and sides of a 24–26 cm (9½–10¼ in) square cake tin and line with baking paper.

To make the filling, place the ricotta in a large bowl and mix well with a spoon to remove all lumps. Add the remaining ingredients and mix together until homogenous. Set aside.

Place the batter ingredients in another bowl and mix with a spoon until well combined. The batter should be easily spreadable, so add a bit more milk if needed.

Spoon just under half the batter into the cake tin, spreading it evenly. Spoon all the ricotta filling evenly over the batter, so that it almost touches the edge of the tin, then flatten it with the back of a spoon. Pour on the remaining batter so that it evenly covers the ricotta and fills in the small gap around the inner perimeter of the cake tin. Tap slightly on the bench if needed to even out the cake batter.

Bake for about 50 minutes, or until golden on top and firm to touch.

Allow to cool completely in the cake tin, before inverting to remove.

The ricotta cake is lovely cold or at room temperature, and will keep in an airtight container in the fridge for about 3 days.

Cherries and chocolate are made for each other and come together in this spiced *focaccia nera* (black cake), based on a recipe by Caterina Prato in her book, *Manuale di Cucina per Principianti e per Cuoche Già Pratiche* ('Cooking manual for beginners and experienced cooks'). A popular book, it was written for home cooks rather than chefs, and was originally written in German (in 1858) – by Katharina Prato, born in Graz. Given the extension of the Austro–Hungarian empire through Trieste and the Istrian peninsula and beyond, it was also translated into Italian, with parts rewritten to make it more relevant to Italian home cooks, and published with an Italianisation of the author's name. The book also influenced other local cookbook authors; books by Marchesa Eta Polesini (1930s) and Maria Stelvio (1942) contain several recipes inspired by Caterina Prato.

I feel very fortunate to have an original edition of the book in Italian, published in 1893. Some of the language used in the book is quite old fashioned, and some of the pages are loose, but I treasure it, wondering who owned the book before me and where they lived. Although my grandmother was married, had children and lived in Pola/Pula for many years, she was born in Klagenfurt, Austria to an Austrian father and an Italian mother. I love to think that this was a cake she used to make, using Istrian sour cherries, chocolate and spices – and that she maybe even owned Caterina Prato's book.

Spiced chocolate & sour cherry cake
(Focaccia nera alle visciole)

Serves 12

680 g (1½ lb) jar of pitted sour
 (Morello) cherries
70 g (2½ oz) raw almonds
100 g (3½ oz) dark chocolate
 (45% cocoa solids)
150 g (1 cup) plain (all-purpose)
 flour
1 teaspoon baking powder
1 teaspoon ground cinnamon
½ teaspoon ground nutmeg
¼ teaspoon ground cloves
sea salt
120 g (4½ oz) unsalted butter,
 softened
120 g (4½ oz) caster sugar
3 eggs
zest of ½ orange
1 teaspoon pure vanilla extract
icing (confectioners') sugar,
 to serve
whipped cream, to serve
 (optional)

Preheat the oven to 150°C (300°F) fan-forced. Line the base and side of a 22 cm (8¾ in) round cake tin with baking paper. (I use a springform tin for this cake.)

Place the cherries in a strainer and strain the juice into a bowl. Set aside.

Place the almonds (including the skin) in a mini processor and process into a flour. Grate the chocolate, using the coarsest side of a box grater.

Place the ground almonds in a large bowl with the flour, baking powder, cinnamon, nutmeg, cloves and a good pinch of salt. Give a quick whisk to combine.

Using a stand mixer with the whisk attached, beat the butter and sugar until creamy. Add the eggs, one at a time, beating well after each addition.

Stir in the flour mixture, grated chocolate, orange zest, vanilla and 3–4 tablespoons of the reserved juice from the jar of cherries. Stir until well combined.

Add the strained cherries and stir them through the batter. The batter should be quite thick, but if it seems too stiff, add a bit more liquid from the jar of cherries. Carefully pour the batter into the cake tin, then tap the tin lightly on the bench to flatten the top of the batter.

Bake for 50–55 minutes, or until a skewer inserted comes out clean. Leave to cool for 10 minutes before releasing from the tin.

Serve at room temperature, dusted with icing sugar; if you are feeling indulgent, enjoy with a side of whipped cream.

My mother was known for her apple strudel, with a pastry stretched so thinly that you can read letters through it. Strudel has Austrian origins but can be found throughout northern Italy, Slovenia, Croatia, the Czech Republic – in fact all the countries that were part of the Austro–Hungarian empire. In Istria it is popularly made with cherries, apples or apricots, making it a dessert you can enjoy in any season. My mother always made the pastry with olive oil, but Maria Stelvio, in her book *La Cucina Triestina*, suggests using softened butter in place of olive oil, and has a particular technique for working the dough (kneading with only the fingertips for 20 minutes, then throwing the dough quite hard on the table several times before kneading further). She even suggests that it does not matter what wet ingredients you have in the dough (oil, butter, whole egg, egg yolk or just water) – it is the method of working and then rolling out the dough that is important.

Apricot strudel
(Strucolo con le albicocche)

Serves 12

For the pastry

180 g (1¼ cups) plain (all-
   purpose) flour, plus extra
   for dusting
sea salt
30 g (1 oz) unsalted butter,
   softened

To make the pastry, place the flour in a bowl with a pinch of salt, giving it a good whisk to combine. Make a well in the centre and add 105 ml (3½ fl oz) of water and the butter. Stir with a spoon until well combined. Tip the pastry onto a floured work surface. Initially, knead with your fingertips until the pastry no longer sticks to your fingers, then knead with the heel of your hand for at least 10 minutes. Don't be tempted to add extra flour – the dough will be very smooth, soft and supple. Place in a clean bowl, cover with a lid or upturned plate and leave to rest for 30 minutes while you prepare the filling.

To make the filling, wash, dry and quarter the apricots, removing the stones. In a large frying pan that can hold all the apricots, melt the butter over medium heat. Add the apricots and sprinkle with the vanilla and half the sugar. Cook for 5–8 minutes, stirring frequently, until the apricots soften and start to release their juices; the time will depend on the size and ripeness of the apricots. Set aside in a sieve to cool completely, draining and discarding any excess liquid (or you could drink the buttery apricot syrup, it is delicious!).

Preheat the oven to 170°C (345°F) fan-forced. Line a large baking sheet with baking paper (ideally the baking sheet should have very low or no sides, so you can easily slip the strudel on and off).

Dust a clean tea towel or tablecloth measuring at least 60 cm x 70 cm (24 in x 28 in) with flour, ready to work with.

To roll out the pastry dough, dust your work surface with flour and gently roll the dough into a rectangle with a rolling pin, flipping it over regularly, and

For the filling

1 kg (2 lb 3 oz) ripe apricots
40 g (1½ oz) unsalted butter
1 teaspoon pure vanilla extract
115 g (½ cup) caster sugar
30 g (1 oz) dry breadcrumbs
60 g (½ cup) flaked almonds
65 g (2¼ oz) unsalted butter

To finish

1 egg yolk, beaten with
    1 teaspoon milk

dusting the surface with more flour as you go, so the delicate dough does not stick and tear.

Once the dough is about 30 cm x 40 cm (12 in x 16 in), carefully lift it onto your prepared tea towel or tablecloth.

Now finish stretching the dough by hand, by carefully placing your hands under the pastry sheet and gently stretching any sections that look thicker. Your sheet needs to be at least 50 cm x 60 cm (20 in x 24 in). If it is any smaller than this, you haven't stretched it thinly enough – you should be able to easily read through the pastry. When you are ready to assemble the strudel, turn the pastry so a shorter edge is closest to you. Trim any thick edges and set them aside (you may need them later).

The filling will cover about one-quarter of the pastry, along the whole shorter length, leaving about 4 cm (1½ in) of pastry free at each end. The other three-quarters of the pastry should have no filling on it.

Melt 35 g (1¼ oz) of the butter and brush it over the entire surface of the pastry. Scatter 1 heaped tablespoon of the breadcrumbs over the part of the pastry where the filling will go. Pile the cooled drained apricots on top of the breadcrumbs. Melt the remaining 30 g (1 oz) butter in a small saucepan; remove from the heat, stir in the remaining breadcrumbs and spoon on top of the apricot filling, followed by the remaining sugar (you may like to adjust the quantity, depending on how sweet your apricots are) and the flaked almonds.

Starting from the edge of pastry that has the filling, use the tea towel to help you roll the strudel into a long sausage enclosing the filling, a little at a time, taking care not to roll it too tightly. When the strudel has been rolled completely, carefully transfer it to your baking sheet (the easiest way to do this is to roll it onto the tray), shaping it into a horse-shoe shape. Brush the outer surface of the pastry with some of the egg wash.

Bake for 10 minutes, then carefully remove from the oven and brush with more egg wash.

Reduce the oven temperature to 160°C (320°F) fan-forced. Bake for a further 25–30 minutes, until the top of the strudel is deeply golden. If you think it is darkening too quickly, drop the temperature to 150°C (300°F) for the last 15–20 minutes. Don't be too alarmed if some of the filling breaks through the pastry.

Remove from the oven and allow to cool completely. The pastry softens over time, and is easier to slice once cooled. The strudel will last for several days in an airtight container, in a cool spot in your kitchen, or the fridge.

THE HOUSE WAS FILLED WITH THE SCENT OF SWEET EASTER BREAD

Author Guido Miglia's memories of Istria are poignant; of younger years spent in the place of his birth, never realising what he would one day lose because of the war. His short stories are beautifully written fragments of times long gone, many set in his home town of Pola: climbing the stone wall to peer into his godfather's backyard to ask for a few stalks of rosemary for his mother's Sunday roast; the smooth stone steps that led to his front door, their heat warming his feet on a balmy summer evening; his mother hurriedly preparing a simple breakfast of bread slices topped with jam, or lard and sugar, before he and his siblings would race out on bicycles towards the beach.

I learned that he lived in a street very close to my father's, not far from the Roman Arena. Guido describes the pomegranate tree in the front garden of his uncle's house, in via Petilia, its pretty red fruit ('*pomi granai*') contrasting vividly against the sea of white houses in the neighbourhood. I like to imagine he and my father knew each other, even if only to nod to say hello, and that many of the descriptions of everyday life in his short stories mirror those of my father and his family in their own house in via Petilia.

Guido's description of the excitement surrounding the preparations for Easter and the Easter Sunday picnic is especially evocative. The field at the front of the house where Guido lived with his family was where shepherds would bring their lambs to sell to locals for Easter celebrations. He remembers holding his mother's hand as they emerged from their home, into a sea of enthusiastic children, bleating lambs and women, all there for the common task of selecting and then bartering for the lamb for the upcoming feast. By Easter eve, the excitement was building and the house was filled with the scent of *pinze* (sweet Easter bread), which were wrapped in a woollen blanket to keep them warm.

On the Sunday morning, the extended family would meet in the Siana forest. Guido remembers wearing his new patent leather shoes for the special day, so tight they made his feet hurt as they walked along the forest path, the scent of the first violets that peeked through the ivy filling the air. Guido's mother would lay down the picnic blanket in the field behind the church of the Madonna of Siana, her bags laden with fragrant *pinze*, hard-boiled eggs dyed red, *titole* (plaited Easter bread made with the *pinza* dough) and fried lamb. And after the feast, the children would dart about between the nearby trestle tables set up for the town's Easter fete, with water guns, home-made shotputs with coloured paper balls, and blow yellow canary-shaped whistles while the blackbirds pecked under the tables, looking for crumbs left over from the feast.

(Guido's recollections liberally translated from *Istria: I Sentieri Della Memoria* by Guido Miglia)

La casa era inondata
dal profumo delle pinze

Easter festivities are not the same without a *pinza*, the traditional Easter cake of the Istrian peninsula. It is more like a sweetened crumbly yeasted bread than a cake, made with eggs, citrus zest, grappa or white rum, and a lengthy proofing time. With the movement of populations and cultures, recipes also travel; you will find *osterpinza* in Vienna, as well as in Trieste, Gorizia, in parts of Slovenia and along the Dalmatian coast. It is often called *pinza Triestina* and should not be confused with an entirely different *pinza* found in Veneto and Trentino–Alto Adige – a heavier denser cake with nuts and dried fruit.

My recipe is based on a *pinza* by Vesna Guštin Grilanc. Scented and delicious, even though it is a sweet bread, it is lovely served with lightly smoked ham or just on its own, as we ate it at home. The incisions on the top of the *pinza* make it look a bit like a flower that has opened its petals.

Sweet Easter bread
(Pinza)

Makes 1 large loaf

500 g (3⅓ cups) plain (all-purpose) flour, plus extra for dusting
2 teaspoons instant dried yeast
115 g (½ cup) caster sugar
190 ml (6½ fl oz) milk
100 g (3½ oz) unsalted butter, melted then cooled
1 egg
2 egg yolks (reserve one of the egg whites for brushing)
1 teaspoon pure vanilla extract
sea salt
zest of 1 small lemon
zest of 1 small orange

To make the dough, place the flour, yeast and sugar in a large wide bowl and whisk to combine. Warm the milk in a saucepan or in the microwave until it is tepid (not hot, or it will destroy the yeast). Place the milk, butter, egg, egg yolks and vanilla in a jug and whisk to combine. Pour into the dry ingredients and stir with a spoon until the dough starts coming together. Add a good pinch of salt, the lemon and orange zest and start kneading, initially in the bowl (it will be quite sticky), then on a well-floured surface. Knead for about 10 minutes, adding a bit more flour if it continues to stick to your hands, but keep in mind that it is a soft dough that will continue to firm up as you knead. (You can also make the dough in a stand mixer using a dough hook.)

Rest the dough in a covered container in a warm draught-free spot for about 2 hours, or until doubled in size.

Knock down the dough and shape it into a ball by folding it onto itself. Place on a baking tray lined with baking paper, seam side down. Cover with a large upturned bowl and place in a warm draught-free spot for 1 hour.

Preheat the oven to 140°C (285°F) fan-forced. Carefully make three incisions in the top of the *pinza* to make a Y-shape, to a depth of about 3 cm (1¼ in). Brush the beaten egg white over the top.

Bake for 40–45 minutes, until the loaf has turned a deep golden and a skewer inserted comes out clean. Place on a wire rack and allow to cool for at least 30 minutes before slicing. Your *pinza* will keep in an airtight container in the pantry for a day or two. It does dry out slightly, so you might like to heat it, or toast it if eating the next day.

My uncle Mario's family was from Buie/Buje, a hilltop town that still has a very Italian feel. The family moved to Monfalcone in the aftermath of the war, which is where he met and married my mother's sister Clara. They made a handsome couple walking arm in arm on the streets of Monfalcone in the late 1940s. In a photo from the era he is on a Vespa, looking a bit like James Dean. A school teacher by trade, Mario was a font of knowledge, with a deep-seated love of books about history and politics, and an inveterate card player. He also loved a joke and was lots of fun to be around, even into his 90s. His elder sister Zoe was a star baker, and was well known for her cakes, especially *putizza*, a spiral brioche-like cake with nuts and dried fruit. She had learned to make *putizza* from her mother Eugenia, who was from Fiume/Rijeka. Every year in the lead-up to Christmas, Zoe would spend several days baking so that she could give cakes to family and friends as a gift, including to her younger brother and his wife, Clara.

My dough recipe is based on the same recipe I use for *pinza* (page 185). In addition to walnuts and sultanas, the filling in my version includes bitter cocoa, cinnamon and orange zest, which apart from the cinnamon, follows my mother's recipe; I am sure signorina Zoe (Miss Zoe, which is what we children politely called her, as she never married) would have approved. This cake has a very Christmassy feel, but don't let that stop you from making it any time of year – I love nothing better than to have it with my coffee, for breakfast or morning tea, during the cooler months.

Yeasted spiral cake
(Putizza)

Serves 12–14

For the filling

150 g (1¼ cups) sultanas
   (golden raisins)
grappa or rum, enough to soak
   the sultanas
400 g (4 cups) walnuts
150 g (5½ oz) honey
zest of 1 orange
1 tablespoon Dutch
   (unsweetened) cocoa powder
1½ teaspoons ground cinnamon
2 egg whites
a few tablespoons milk
   (as needed)
sea salt

For the dough

500 g (3⅓ cups) plain (all-
   purpose) flour, plus extra
   for dusting
2 teaspoons instant dried
   yeast
115 g (½ cup) caster sugar
190 ml (6½ fl oz) milk
100 g (3½ oz) unsalted butter,
   melted then cooled, plus extra
   for greasing
1 egg
2 egg yolks
1 teaspoon pure vanilla extract
sea salt
zest of 1 lemon

For brushing

1 egg yolk, beaten with a dash
   of milk

To make the filling, soak the sultanas in grappa or rum, covering them so they are immersed. Do this the day before, if possible, otherwise at least 1 hour before using.

To make the dough, place the flour, yeast and sugar in a large wide bowl and whisk to combine. Warm the milk in a saucepan or in the microwave until it is tepid (not hot, or it will destroy the yeast). Place the milk, butter, egg, egg yolks and vanilla in a jug and whisk to combine. Pour into the dry ingredients and stir with a spoon until the dough starts coming together. Add a good pinch of salt and the lemon zest and start kneading, initially in the bowl (it will be quite sticky), then on a well-floured surface. Knead for about 10 minutes, adding a bit more flour if it continues to stick to your hands, but keep in mind that it is a soft dough that will continue to firm up as you knead. (You can also make the dough in a stand mixer using a dough hook.)

Rest the dough in a covered container in a warm draught-free spot for about 2 hours, or until doubled in size.

While the dough is resting, make the filling. Place the walnuts in a food processor and grind them to a medium-fine crumb. Tip into a large bowl. Add the drained sultanas and the remaining ingredients, except the milk. Also add a good pinch of salt. The filling needs to be a thick, spreadable paste, so add a bit of milk if needed. Set aside.

Grease the base and side of a 26 cm (10¼ in) round cake tin (mine has a removable base), then line with baking paper.

Flour your work surface and roll out the dough with a rolling pin so that it measures about 40 x 60 cm (16 in x 24 in). Spread the filling on the dough, leaving a border of about 8 cm (3¼ in) along one of the long edges, and 2 cm (¾ in) on the other three sides.

Starting on the long edge with the 2 cm (¾ in) border, roll the dough into a sausage. Shape into a loose spiral, then carefully lift into the cake tin. Cover with a clean tea towel and rest for 45 minutes in a warm spot.

Preheat the oven to 150°C (300°F) fan-forced. Brush the top of the loaf with the egg wash and bake for about 10 minutes.

Reduce the oven temperature to 140°C (285°F) and bake for 45–50 minutes, or until the top of the cake is deep golden and a skewer inserted comes out clean.

Place on a wire rack and allow to cool completely, for at least 1 hour, before slicing.

Your *putizza* will keep in an airtight container in a cool place for 2–3 days.

My mother often spoke of *pan de fighi* (fig bread). Her mother would send her to the town bakery with a loaf of uncooked bread, ready to bake in the communal oven. The ladies in the bakery would give her some fig bread to munch on while she waited. I became obsessed with trying to replicate these memories for my mother and found a version of *pan de fighi* recounted in an online video by Serafino Bencic, from Lisignano/Ližnjan on the southern tip of the Istrian peninsula. He speaks in Istrian–Venetian dialect and describes the *pan de fighi* that he remembers eating in his family home. He muses on his childhood breakfast during autumn: a bunch of grapes, a piece of bread and a few figs. His family would preserve the figs to eat through the year by breaking them in half and laying them out on the table to dry. When they had dried, they would be minced and made into a paste that would then be mixed in with bread dough and baked into *pan de fighi*. Serafino says the bread was delicious, and his family would eat fig bread instead of plain bread and jam.

I made this recipe many times while testing it, initially just with figs, but then adding another ingredient in the next version. In the end there were walnuts, rosemary and orange zest in my fig bread. It is a lot fancier than Serafino's description, but uses ingredients that complement each other so well. I am sure he would love it as much as you will – and as much as my mother did; she was my taste tester for this recipe.

Fig & walnut loaf
(Pan de fighi)

Serves 12–14

480 g (3½ cups) plain (all-
    purpose) flour, plus extra
    for dusting
55 g (¼ cup) caster sugar
10 g (⅓ oz) instant dried yeast
240 ml (8 fl oz) lukewarm milk
60 ml (¼ cup) extra virgin
    olive oil
30 g (1 oz) unsalted butter,
    melted then cooled, plus extra
    for greasing
¾ teaspoon fine sea salt
zest of 1 small orange
1 tablespoon fresh rosemary
    leaves, finely chopped
220 g (8 oz) dried figs
boiling water (if needed)
60 g (⅔ cup) chopped walnuts
1 small egg, whisked with a
    dash of milk (for brushing)

Place the flour, sugar and yeast in a large bowl and whisk to combine. In a jug, mix the milk, olive oil and butter together with a spoon. Make a well in the centre of your dry ingredients and pour in the milky mixture. Stir with a wooden spoon, then bring together with your hands.

Tip onto a lightly floured work surface and work the dough for 1 minute. Add the salt, orange zest and rosemary, then knead for about 10 minutes, or until smooth and elastic.

Place the dough in a bowl, cover with a large upturned plate and rest in a warm draught-free spot for 2 hours, or until almost doubled in size. While the dough is resting, remove the hard stem from the figs (if present) and chop the fruit into small pieces. If the figs are on the firm side, place the pieces in a bowl with a cup of boiling water for 10 minutes to soften them. Drain well and leave to partially dry out.

Grease the sides of a large loaf (bar) tin and line with baking paper. My tin measures about 10 cm x 22 cm (4 in x 8¾ in), with 10 cm (4 in) sides.

Roll out your dough until it is the size of a large rectangle, with one length the same length as your loaf tin. Sprinkle the walnut and fig pieces evenly over the dough. Roll it up to enclose the fruit and nuts (you don't need to be too precise) and place in the tin.

Cover with a clean tea towel and allow to rest another 30 minutes.

Preheat the oven to 160°C (320°F) fan-forced. Brush the top of the bread with the egg wash, then bake for 45 minutes, or until golden brown. If it is browning too quickly, drop the temperature to 150°C (300°F).

Enjoy warm or at room temperature. After a couple of days, if you still have any left, toast thick slices and serve spread with butter.

My friend Ksenija calls her grandmother on her father's side *baka* ('grandmother' in Croatian). Ksenija's *baka* left a legacy of recipes, including her Hungarian cake. I tried the cake when we went to Ksenija's home in the centre of Pola/Pula for a late breakfast one sunny Sunday morning. As we were heading back to Trieste by bus later that day, Ksenija had told me she was sending us off with a substantial breakfast, like the one they might have on Easter Sunday morning. We thought we might have a coffee on arrival – but in true Istrian style, we were served home-infused grappa with carob pods. What followed was an antipasto-style feast with local cured meats, cheeses, pickled vegetables and bread. We finished off the feast with a four-layered cake, spread with a chocolate cream between the layers. It was richly delicious, and the layering was perfect. Ksenija explained that this is what her baka called Hungarian cake; I later found out it is based on the *Dobos torte* from Hungary, first created in the late 1800s in Budapest. The typical version has seven cake layers, chocolate buttercream layers and a firm caramel topping.

I have followed Ksenija's grandmother's lead and made a rectangular four-layer cake, using the same chocolate buttercream as the icing. In a nod to my love for the combination of chocolate and orange, I have used orange zest and juice in place of the more traditional lemon. Making the cake is relatively simple, though the assembly takes a bit of patience. The size of my cake was guided by the size of my baking trays and my lidded storage container. It can be made round, or like a log. The choice is yours. It is a rather rich cake, so one slice is plenty!

Baka's Hungarian layer cake
(Torta di baka)

Serves 12–16

For the cake

6 eggs, at room temperature

140 g (⅔ cup) caster (superfine) sugar

1 tablespoon freshly squeezed orange juice

160 g (5½ oz) plain (all-purpose) flour

1 teaspoon orange zest

sea salt

candied orange peel, for decorating

For the chocolate buttercream

220 g (8 oz) unsalted butter, at room temperature, plus extra for greasing

1 tablespoon white rum

1 tablespoon milk, plus a bit extra if needed

1 teaspoon vanilla bean paste (or the scraped seeds of a vanilla pod)

155 g (1¼ cups) icing (confectioners') sugar, sifted

55 g (½ cup) Dutch (unsweetened) cocoa powder

Preheat the oven to 160°C (320°F) fan-forced. Rub a bit of butter over two baking trays, then top each with a sheet of baking paper. My baking trays measured 33 cm x 28 cm (13¼ in x 11 in).

To make the cake, separate the eggs, placing the yolks in the bowl of a stand mixer and the whites in a separate clean bowl. Add the sugar to the egg yolks, together with the orange juice, and beat on medium speed until thick and creamy. Add the flour, orange zest and a pinch of salt and beat for a couple of minutes until combined; the mixture will be pale and quite thick.

Add a pinch of salt to the egg whites and whisk (by hand, or with electric beaters) until stiff peaks form.

Add a heaped tablespoon of egg white to the cake batter and mix to loosen it a little. In batches, carefully fold the remaining egg white into the batter, being careful not to lose aeration.

Divide the mixture into two and evenly spread half the batter on one baking tray and half on the other tray, so that they almost reach the edges and are the same size.

Bake for 8–9 minutes, or until cooked through and golden.

Remove the first cake sheet from the oven and carefully invert onto a large wire cake rack. Carefully peel off the baking paper, then flip the cake back over, onto a clean sheet of baking paper. Repeat with the second cake.

Cut each sheet of cake in half (or into three if you would like to make a six-layer cake); my four cake pieces measured 14 cm x 24 cm (5½ in x 9½ in). Set aside to cool completely (it won't take long).

To make the chocolate buttercream – dice the butter and place in the bowl of your stand mixer. Beat on medium speed for 1 minute until smooth, then add the rum, milk and vanilla. In batches (so the powder doesn't fly everywhere!), add the icing sugar and cocoa. Beat until homogenous. The buttercream will be thick but easily spreadable; if it isn't, add a bit more milk.

To assemble the cake – place one layer of cake on a clean sheet of baking paper, cut slightly larger than the cake. Using a spatula, carefully and evenly spread about one-fifth of the buttercream over the cake. Carefully place another layer of cake on top, then spread on another one-fifth of the buttercream. Repeat until the cake is stacked with all four layers. Spread the remaining buttercream on the sides and ends of the assembled cake so that it is completely covered. Decorate the top with candied orange peel.

Using a thin transfer board, slide the completed cake, with the baking paper, into a sufficiently large lidded container that you can place in the fridge.

Refrigerate for at least 2 hours (and up to 2 days) before serving.

As Francesco Gottardi writes, some cakes were not everyday cakes. They might be made to show off a bit when you were expecting guests, so he calls them *dolci da esibizione* (cakes to put on show). This is one of them – and along with Baka's Hungarian layer cake (page 194), it is one of my favourite 'on show' cakes. In true Hapsburg style, the cake is cut into layers and sandwiched together with buttercream, in this case a coffee buttercream.

As I rarely make such fancy cakes, and do not have any special cake decorating equipment; I use a butter knife to place and smooth on the buttercream, which sits on a dinner plate while I do it. So this is quite a humble version, but it tastes very good, especially if you use good-quality extra-strong espresso made with a mocha. Please do not be tempted to use instant coffee.

Almond & coffee cake
(Torta di mandorle e caffè)

Serves 12

For the cake

145 g (⅔ cup) caster sugar
6 eggs, at room temperature, separated
30 g (¼ cup) plain (all-purpose) flour
180 g (1¾ cups) almond meal
1 teaspoon pure vanilla extract
sea salt
whole coffee beans, to decorate (optional)

For the coffee buttercream

120 g (4½ oz) unsalted butter, softened, plus extra for greasing
120 g (1 cup) icing (confectioners') sugar
1 teaspoon pure vanilla extract
60 ml (¼ cup) strong black coffee, at room temperature

Preheat the oven to 150°C (300°F) fan-forced. Grease the base and side of a 21 cm (8¼ in) round cake tin with a removable base, then line with baking paper.

To make the cake, beat the sugar and egg yolks using a stand mixer with the whisk attached until pale, thick and creamy. Add the flour, almond meal, vanilla and a pinch of salt and mix until well combined.

In a separate clean bowl, whisk the egg whites with a pinch of salt (by hand, or with electric beaters) until stiff peaks form. Add a heaped tablespoon of egg white to the cake batter and mix to loosen it a little. In batches, carefully fold the remaining egg white into the batter, being careful not to lose aeration.

Carefully pour the batter into the cake tin, then bake for 40–45 minutes, or until a skewer inserted comes out clean. Set aside to cool completely. Once cooled, cut the cake evenly into two layers.

To make the coffee buttercream, beat the butter and icing sugar using your stand mixer on medium speed for at least 5 minutes, until smooth and creamy. Add the vanilla and 1 tablespoon of coffee at a time, beating well after each addition until incorporated.

Spread some of the buttercream over the bottom cake layer, then sandwich the other cake half on top. Spread the remaining buttercream over the top and the side of the cake. Decorate the top of the cake with whole coffee beans, if you like. Place the cake in a sealed container in a cool spot for a few hours to allow the buttercream to firm up. Cut into slices using a very sharp knife.

Keep the cake in the sealed container in the fridge and eat within 4 days.

Mamma used to make two different cakes with crumble toppings: one with apples and one with plums. The apple one had a topping that included granola, but the plum one was my favourite. The texture and acidity of the plums and the sweetness of crumbly topping made it both comforting and delicious, especially when eaten warm. We would pick plums at the end of summer from the trees in the backyard, make plum jam, stew a good portion of them and bake this cake many times over. I cannot be sure, but I think Mamma learned it from one of the Istrian ladies who went to the social club she and my father used to visit. This type of crumble topping over fruit and a cake base makes it a streusel cake, with roots firmly embedded in Germanic culture, rather than a crumble.

Plum cake with a streusel topping
(Torta con susine)

Serves 12

100 g (3½ oz) unsalted butter, at room temperature
80 g (⅓ cup) caster sugar
2 eggs
75 g (½ cup) spelt flour
75 g (½ cup) plain (all-purpose) flour
1 heaped teaspoon baking powder
60 ml (¼ cup) milk
1 teaspoon pure vanilla extract
sea salt
500 g (1 lb 2 oz) plums
1 heaped tablespoon raw sugar

For the crunchy topping

40 g (1½ oz) spelt flour
40 g (1½ oz) unsalted butter, chilled and finely diced
1½ tablespoons raw sugar
40 g (⅓ cup) walnuts

Preheat the oven to 160°C (320°F) fan-forced. Grease the base and side of a 22 cm (8¾ in) round springform baking tin, then line with baking paper.

Using a stand mixer with the whisk attached, beat the butter and sugar for a few minutes, until well combined. Add the eggs, one at a time, scraping down the side of the bowl as needed. Once well combined, add the flours, baking powder, milk, vanilla and a pinch of salt, then beat again until well combined. The mixture will be quite thick.

Spoon the batter into the cake tin. Slice open the plums and remove the stones, then cut each plum into eighths. Place the plum pieces on top of the batter, so they form an even layer. Sprinkle the raw sugar over the top.

Place the topping ingredients, except the walnuts, in a bowl. Add a pinch of salt and, using your fingers, crumble the mixture together. Finely chop the walnuts, then toss them through the crumble mixture. Sprinkle the lot over the plums.

Bake for about 50 minutes; the cake will be ready when the topping is brown, and a skewer inserted comes out clean (and the kitchen smells delicious).

Allow to cool for 5–10 minutes before removing from the tin. Serve warm or at room temperature. The cake will last for a few days in a cool spot in a sealed container.

Whenever we visit Pola/Pula, we catch up with our friends Ksenija and Tomica for a long lunch. 'Lunch' is probably a bit of a stretch, as it is usually after 4 pm. We go to a different *konoba* (Croatian for 'restaurant') every time, always a traditional and generous place that has sometimes opened just for us. The meal will continue until at least 7 pm, and course after course of delicious home-made dishes will appear. I never quite know what Ksenija says to the owners of the restaurant, but we get special treatment every time. The cook always comes out to talk to us, to explain (sometimes in Croatian, with a mix of English or Istrian–Venetian dialect) what we are eating.

This dish is inspired by one such meal in Valle/Bale in 2017. The cook's speciality, so she told me, was pasta. So we ate potato gnocchi, *fusi* and many other dishes which, given the passage of time, I no longer remember. I do however remember the dessert: *palacinche* (crepes), rolled up and stuffed with berries, served warm, topped with ice cream. For the recipe below I have used mamma Lina's *palacinche* recipe (page 258), which is slightly sweet and fragrant from the inclusion of orange and lemon zest in the batter. I use blood oranges for this recipe, which are less sweet and a deep red colour, but feel free to use regular oranges.

Crepes with cherries, orange & cinnamon
(Palacinche con ciliege)

Serves 4 generously

900 g (2 lb) pitted cherries (fresh or frozen)
200 ml (7 fl oz) freshly squeezed orange juice, ideally from blood oranges
100 ml (3½ fl oz) white rum
80 g (⅓ cup) caster sugar
2 cinnamon sticks
8 Lina's crepes (page 258), warmed
vanilla ice cream, to serve

If using frozen cherries, let them thaw. Place the cherries, orange juice, rum, sugar and cinnamon sticks in a saucepan over medium heat. Once the liquid comes to the boil, reduce the heat and simmer, uncovered and stirring occasionally, for 10 minutes. Remove the cherries with a slotted spoon and place in a strainer to remove the excess liquid (collect this and put it back in your saucepan).

Continue cooking the collected liquid at a simmer until it reduces and thickens, about 15 minutes. Remove from the heat and remove the cinnamon sticks.

Distribute the drained cherries evenly on one edge of the slightly warmed crepes, reserving a few for garnish. Roll each crepe up into a cigar that wraps around the cherries.

Drizzle on the syrup, top with ice cream and garnish with the reserved cherries. Serve immediately.

STORIES TOLD OVER BLACK AND WHITE PHOTOS, HANDWRITTEN RECIPES AND APPLE CAKE

My father knew Bibo from Pola. They lived a few streets from each other, not far the Roman Arena. Bibo had gone to school with my aunt Nives, my godmother Gemma and my uncle Mario, and although my father was a few years older and they weren't close friends, they knew of each other. They reconnected in Melbourne, in 1950. I only recently found out the story of their meeting when I caught up with Jolanda, Bibo's sprightly widow, in early 2020. She is from Abbazia on the west coast of the Istrian peninsula, a resort town of Hapsburg-era villas.

Jolanda's daughter Samantha had arranged for us to meet at her apartment, as she knew I was writing a cookbook about Istria. Jolanda, or Jole for short, has a formidable memory and we chatted in dialect for several hours, recounting many stories over black and white photos, old recipes, and an apple cake that Samantha had made using her paternal grandmother Anita's recipe. The recipe was in a handwritten recipe book – an heirloom with page after page of dessert recipes, including a total of ten apple cakes. After leafing through Anita's recipe book, Jole told me the story of how my father first met Bibo here in Melbourne.

My father, Nello, had arrived in Australia in May 1950 on the *General Greeley*. As a sponsored migrant, he and my mother, upon landing at Station Pier, were shuttled immediately onto a train and sent far into the Australian countryside, to a former army camp called Bonegilla. They stayed there, enduring the terrible food in the camp's canteen (mutton was a regular on the menu, often boiled). My parents must have had a premonition that the food would be terrible, as they had brought a tiny camping stove with them from Italy.

They enjoyed the occasional picnics with fellow *istriani* Stanco, Emma, Ernesto and Antonietta, flaunting the rules and cooking outdoors. Their stay in Bonegilla was thankfully just over a month, and once they were placed in factory jobs, they were moved to Melbourne, to a camp in the bayside suburb of Williamstown. The camping stove got another workout there as the food was apparently not a lot better, and was eventually confiscated, as the walls in their sleeping quarters were paper-thin and a fire risk. But food was not the only thing they missed.

The Williamstown camp was close to Station Pier, the port of arrival of their ship. It was a place my father liked to revisit, turning up to greet as many ships from Italy as his work schedule would allow, on the slim chance that he might know one of the new arrivals. I like to imagine the hope in his heart, as he waited, wearing his hat, holding his pipe, looking for a thread of connection on this Australian shore to his Istrian homeland.

One day in August 1950 he went to Station Pier, as the *Fairsea* had just docked. As he watched the line of European passengers disembark onto Australian soil, he spotted a familiar face. Bibo and Nello hugged and quickly exchanged stories of their movements after they left Istria, and of their respective month-long ocean journeys. My father excitedly described the opportunities there were in Australia: jobs, land to build a house, space to grow a garden, and a bay full of fish.

And to start Bibo off in his new country, Nello handed him two shillings. New money, for a new future, for their lives as 'new' Australians, so far from home.

*Storie raccontate attraverso foto in
bianco e nero, ricette scritte a mano
e torta di mele*

The recipe for this cake is from nonna Nita's handwritten recipe book. I was lucky enough to see Nita's heirloom recipe diary when I spent an afternoon with Signora Jolanda, the widow of Bibo (a close friend of my father's from Pola/Pula), and her daughter Samantha. Anita, or Nita for short, was Samantha's paternal grandmother, a regal-looking woman with a heart of gold and a love of cooking. This is the cake we shared that afternoon, a deliciously moist apple cake – one of ten in Nita's precious recipe book.

Nita's apple cake
(Torta di mele di nonna Nita)

Serves 12

2 egg yolks, lightly beaten

80 g (⅓ cup) caster sugar

30 g (1 oz) unsalted butter, melted and cooled, plus an extra 20 g (¾ oz) and a little for greasing

200 g (1⅓ cups) plain (all-purpose) flour

2 teaspoons baking powder

150 ml (5 fl oz) milk

125 ml (½ cup) dry white wine

zest of 1 lemon

1 teaspoon pure vanilla extract

sea salt

4 small-medium apples (pink lady, fuji or jonathan), about 600 g (1 lb 5 oz)

2 tablespoons cherry jam

1 tablespoon brandy

30 g (¼ cup) sultanas (golden raisins)

40 g (1½ oz) amaretti biscuits (12–14 biscuits, depending on their size)

icing (confectioners') sugar, for dusting (optional)

Preheat the oven to 160°C (320°F) fan-forced. Grease the base and side of a round 21 cm (8¼ in) springform cake tin, then line with baking paper.

Place the egg yolks, sugar and the 30 g (1 oz) of melted butter in a large bowl. Add the flour, baking powder, milk, wine, lemon zest, vanilla and a pinch of salt. Beat lightly with a whisk to remove any lumps and combine; the mixture will be quite liquid. Leave to rest for 30 minutes while you prepare the other ingredients.

Peel and core the apples. Cut the apples into quarters, and each quarter into segments about 6 mm (¼ in) thick. In a small bowl, mix the jam and brandy until combined.

Pour half the batter into the cake tin. Top with half the apple slices, then dot with half the extra butter. Scatter over the sultanas and the amaretti, crushing them by hand as you go. Add the remaining apple, dot with the remaining butter and drizzle with the jam mixture. Pour on the second layer of cake batter, which will partially sink between the apple slices.

Bake for about 1¼ hours, or until the cake is golden and firm to touch. Check the cake periodically and reduce the oven temperature to 150°C (300°F) if it is browning too quickly.

Wait until the cake cools before removing it from the tin. Serve dusted with icing sugar, if desired.

The cake will keep in a sealed container in a cool spot for up to 3 days.

As soon as I read about these stuffed baked apples in nonna Nita's recipe book, I loved the sound of them – *mele col segreto* ('apples with a secret'). As Nita is no longer with us, I will have to guess which ingredient is the secret one that the title refers to. It could be the prune, which you wouldn't expect to be stuffed in the centre of an apple, but my bets are on the crushed, slightly bitter amaretti, which are hiding under the prune in the heart of the baked apple.

For this recipe you will need sweet apples that are good for baking, like royal gala or sundowner; they should be red apples if you want to be true to nonna Nita's recipe. Dry white wine is the cooking medium, and the alcohol evaporates as the apples cook. If you prefer, you could use water or verjuice as a substitute for the wine.

You can easily halve the recipe for four people, but these baked apples make great leftovers that can be enjoyed the next day. A scoop of vanilla ice cream is optional and quite lovely on a winter's evening if you serve them warm. I prefer them at room temperature. As nonna Nita writes at the end of her recipe, *'sono squisite'* ('they are delicious').

Baked apples with a secret
(Mele col segreto)

Serves 8

8 red medium-sized apples, such as sundowner, royal gala or MiApple
40 g (1½ oz) amaretti biscuits (12–14 biscuits, depending on size)
2 tablespoons apricot jam
8 small prunes, pitted
140 ml (4½ fl oz) dry white wine
60 g (¼ cup) raw sugar

Preheat the oven to 160°C (320°F) fan-forced. Peel part of the skin from the apples in a spiral pattern, leaving some skin intact. Carefully core the apples.

Crush the amaretti to a coarse crumb and mix with the jam. Place a heaped teaspoon of the mixture into each of the cored apples, then fill the remaining space with a prune. Depending on the size of your apples and how much of the centre you remove with the corer, you may need more or less filling mixture.

Place the apples upright in a baking dish in which they will fit easily. Pour the wine into the dish and scatter the sugar over the apples.

Bake for 50–60 minutes, until the apples are cooked through. You can check by squeezing them between your fingers, or with a thin skewer, which should insert quite easily. Allow them to cool in the oven, with the oven turned off, for about 10 minutes.

The sugary syrup in the dish will be quite thick. If you want to reheat it to serve with the apples, scrape it into a saucepan when it is still warm and gently heat.

You can serve the apples warm, with some of the syrup poured on, but they are lovelier at room temperature. Serve with vanilla ice cream, thick cream, or just on their own.

Biscuits to serve with tea or coffee

Biscotti da servire con il tè o il caffè

If you have spent some time in Venice, you may have noticed yellow, often log-shaped, biscuits called *zaleti* in pastry shop windows. As the towns along the west coast of Istria were part of the Republic of Venice for some 500 years, the foods were heavily influenced by those of Venice. In his book *Parenzo: Gente, luoghi, memoria,* Aulo Crisma writes about his memories of Parenzo/Poreç, where he and many generations of his family were born. The Crisma family owned a bakery in via Carducci, and his elder brother Steno was the *panettiere* (or *pec* in dialect; the baker). On Thursdays, Steno would bake biscotti, and the scent of vanilla would waft down the entire length of the street. On Fridays it was the yeasty smell of bread and *saltimpansa* (literally, 'stomach-jumpers' – bread rolls that are brushed with butter and dusted in sugar before baking). On Saturdays it was the buttery goodness of shortcrust pastry and *zaleti* – these sweet yellow polenta biscuits.

Sweet yellow polenta biscuits
(Zaleti)

Makes about 28

4 tablespoons sultanas (golden raisins)

grappa, for soaking the sultanas (optional)

300 g (2 cups) fine instant yellow polenta

200 g (1⅓ cups) plain (all-purpose) flour

2 teaspoons baking powder

100 g (3½ oz) golden caster (superfine) sugar

pinch of fine sea salt

zest of 1 lemon

zest of 1 orange

100 g (3½ oz) unsalted butter

3 eggs, lightly beaten

1 teaspoon pure vanilla extract

3 teaspoons pine nuts or pistachio nuts

Soak the sultanas in grappa (if using) or warm water for 1 hour, then strain, reserving the liquid.

Preheat the oven to 150°C (300°F) fan-forced. Line a baking tray with baking paper.

Place the polenta, flour, baking powder, sugar and salt in a bowl. Whisk briefly to combine, then add the citrus zests. Melt the butter in a small saucepan and add to the dry ingredients. Mix well with a wooden spoon. Add the egg and vanilla extract and mix until everything is evenly incorporated.

Lastly, add the nuts and strained sultanas. (If the mixture appears too dry, add some of the reserved grappa or warm water.)

Shape balls of the dough into apricot-sized lozenges, about 35 g (1¼ oz) each. Place on the baking tray with some space between them, to allow them to spread. Bake for 20–25 minutes, until golden.

Leave to cool on a wire rack. *Zaleti* have a rather crumbly texture, though they will have a bit of crunch if you cook them longer. They are lovely dipped in coffee, or with a glass of liqueur.

They will keep in an airtight container for up to 5 days.

Bussolai are Venetian bread rings, sometimes S-shaped, sometimes shaped like a stick. There are also sweet versions and, given the extent of the Republic of Venice over the ages, it makes sense that there was a version on the eastern shore of the Adriatic Sea in Istria. I was inspired by the version with almond meal and cinnamon described by Marchesa Eta Polesini in her book about what she serves her guests with tea. She calls them *buzolai*, the word *buzo* (or *buso*) being the dialect word for 'hole'. She suggests adding *acquavite* (which literally means 'water of life', but is actually grappa, a grape distillate) to the dough, and dipping them in more *acquavite* after cooking. This would impart quite a strong taste, which I love, but I have suggested rum in its place. And in terms of dipping, tea or coffee would be lovely.

Cinnamon ring biscuits
(Buzolai alla cannella)

Makes about 18

160 g (5½ oz) plain (all-purpose) flour
1 scant teaspoon baking powder
140 g (1⅓ cups) almond meal
1 teaspoon ground cinnamon
sea salt
140 g (5 oz) unsalted butter, at room temperature
70 g (2½ oz) caster (superfine) sugar
1 egg yolk
30 ml (1 fl oz) white rum
zest of 1 lemon

For dusting

2 teaspoons ground cinnamon
1 tablespoon caster (superfine) sugar

Place the flour, baking powder, almond meal and cinnamon in a large bowl with a good pinch of salt. Whisk briefly to combine and remove any lumps. Set aside.

Cut the butter roughly and place in the bowl of an electric stand mixer with the whisk attached. Add the sugar and beat on medium speed for a few minutes, until well combined and creamy. Drop in the egg yolk, rum and lemon zest and briefly beat to combine. Swapping the whisk for a large spoon, stir in the dry ingredients in batches, mixing until well combined. Transfer the dough to an airtight container and allow to rest in the fridge for at least 1 hour.

Preheat the oven to 160°C (320°F) fan-forced. Line two baking trays with baking paper.

Place the extra cinnamon and sugar on a small plate and stir until combined.

Break off 30 g (1 oz) balls (about the size of small apricots) from your rested dough. Roll into ropes about 13 cm (5 in) long, then bring the ends together, to make rings. If the dough is too soft to roll properly, put it in the fridge for another 15 minutes or so.

Dip each ring in the cinnamon sugar and place on the trays, with the dusted side facing up. Place the trays in the fridge for about 10 minutes, so the uncooked biscuits can firm up a bit.

Bake, in batches if needed, for 22 minutes, or until lightly coloured underneath. Allow to cool for a few minutes before removing from the trays, as the biscuits are somewhat fragile when warm, but firm up as they cool down.

They will keep for up to 1 week in an airtight container.

A metal box sat in our pantry at home. It was an old biscuit tin, repurposed into a new biscuit tin – one for home-made biscuits. More often than not, these were crescent-shaped *chifel*, a word borrowed from the German word *kipfel*. Mamma made her *chifel* with almonds and vanilla extract, and eating them transports me back to another time, another place, when the world seemed larger, and the kitchen always smelt good. My father had a real sweet tooth, and not a day went by that he wouldn't request a sweet, even just a small one, to have with his coffee after lunch. And *chifel* fit the bill.

I was inspired by Caterina Prato and her recipe for *bastoncelli all'anice* (aniseed-flavoured finger biscuits), and combined this with Mamma's *chifel* recipe to make aniseed-scented crescents. They are a bit time-consuming to shape, but please persevere, as they have a satisfyingly dense texture, which is typical of Italian breakfast biscuits. I buy aniseed extract from specialty online stores. If you cannot find it, use a splash of Sambuca or other aniseed-flavoured liqueur, and add half a teaspoon crushed or powdered anise seeds to the dough.

Aniseed crescents
(Chifel all'anice)

Makes 18–20

140 g (1⅓ cups) almond meal
140 g (5 oz) caster sugar
140 g (5 oz) plain (all-purpose) flour, plus extra for dusting
sea salt
70 g (2½ oz) unsalted butter, at room temperature, cut into small dice
1 egg, separated
1 teaspoon aniseed extract (or 1 teaspoon Sambuca plus ½ teaspoon crushed anise seeds)

For dusting

1 teaspoon sugar
1 teaspoon crushed anise seeds

Preheat the oven to 140°C (275°F) fan-forced. Line a baking tray with baking paper.

Place the almond meal, sugar, flour and a good pinch of salt in a large bowl and whisk to combine, then rub the butter in with your fingertips until well combined.

Whisk the egg yolk, about half the egg white and the aniseed extract in a small cup, then add to the flour mixture and stir to combine. Bring the dough together with your hands – it will be quite dry, so add a bit more egg white if needed to bring the dough together; just remember to reserve a little for brushing on the crescents before baking.

Flour your work surface. Cut off walnut-sized chunks of dough, about 25 g (1 oz) each. Carefully roll them into logs about 10 cm (4 in) long – they may be a bit crumbly. Carefully shape them into crescents and place on the baking tray. Brush the crescents with the remaining egg white. Combine the extra sugar and crushed anise seeds, then sprinkle onto the crescents.

Bake for 20–22 minutes, until the biscuits are cooked through and turning a golden colour. Allow to cool for 5–10 minutes on the tray, before carefully lifting them onto a wire rack to cool completely.

Aniseed crescents will keep for about 5 days in an airtight container.

When I was in Pisino/Pazin, I stopped at an old-fashioned bakery and, upon entering, said 'Dober dan' ('Good day' in Croatian), quickly followed by *'Parli italiano?'* ('Do you speak Italian?'). Luckily the lady behind the counter did, so I asked if she had any traditional baked goods. She pointed to a sign that said *cukerančići*. The Croatian 'c' sounds quite a bit like an English or Italian 'z'. Italian Istrians call these biscuits *zucherancici*.

It was traditional to bake *zucherancici* for weddings and baptisms. Diagonal incisions are made in strips or rods of dough, using either a knife or a fluted pastry cutter, and the dough is then shaped into a circle, forming a flower or star. They are delicate and delicious. While these sweet celebratory biscuits are still warm from the oven, they are dunked in Malvasia, the local wine, before being dusted with icing sugar. Malvasia is not that easy to find outside Europe, so I brush the freshly baked biscuits with a mix of white rum and grappa. If you prefer, you can omit this step and simply dust with icing sugar.

Istrian wedding biscuits
(Zucherancici or cukerančići)

Makes about 30

400 g (2⅔ cups) plain
  (all-purpose) flour
1 teaspoon baking powder
¼ teaspoon fine sea salt
2 large eggs, at room
  temperature
120 g (½ cup) caster (superfine)
  sugar
½ teaspoon pure vanilla extract
30 ml (1 fl oz) milk, at room
  temperature
2 teaspoons white rum
zest of 1 small lemon
100 g (3½ oz) unsalted butter, at
  room temperature, chopped

To finish

3 teaspoons grappa, for
  brushing
3 teaspoons white rum,
  for brushing
icing (confectioners') sugar,
  for dusting

Place the flour, baking powder and salt in a bowl and whisk briefly to combine. Set aside.

Place the eggs and sugar in the bowl of an electric stand mixer with the whisk attached and beat on medium speed for at least 5 minutes, until light and fluffy. Add the vanilla, milk, rum and lemon zest and mix briefly.

Reduce the speed to low, then add a heaped tablespoon of the flour mixture. Allow it to be incorporated, then add a knob of butter while keeping the motor running. Allow the butter to blend in, then add another heaped tablespoon of the flour mixture. Keep alternating the flour and butter until they are used up; you may need to stop the motor occasionally to scrape down the side of the bowl. The dough will be cohesive but soft.

Scrape the dough out of the bowl and place on a sheet of baking paper. Cover with another sheet of baking paper, then roll out to a thickness of about 8 mm (⅓ in); I made a rectangle approximately 25–30 cm (10–12 in).

Rest the covered and rolled-out dough in a cool spot (or in the fridge if the weather is warm) for about 30 minutes.

Preheat the oven to 180°C (350°F) fan-forced. Line two baking trays with baking paper.

Cut the rested dough into strips about 10 cm (4 in) long and 2–3 cm (¾–1¼ in) wide. Without cutting all the way through, cut four or five incisions along the strips, on the diagonal. Now take the ends of one strip and bring them together, so that it forms a small circle, with spokes pointing outwards. Repeat with the other strips, placing them on the baking trays.

Bake for 10–12 minutes, in batches if needed. The biscuits are ready when they are firm, pale on top and slightly golden underneath.

As soon as you take them out of the oven, brush them with the grappa mixed with the rum, then sprinkle with icing sugar.

Eat once cooled. They will keep for up to 1 week in an airtight container.

A SONG ABOUT A GIRL WHOSE SHOP SOLD EVERYTHING EXCEPT SALTED COD

My first language was not English or Italian, it was *dialetto* (dialect). Sentences peppered with *gho* and *xe* ('have' and 'is' respectively), and distinctly non-Italian words such as *spargher* (stovetop) and *palacinche* (crepes), makes it very much a language of border communities. It is broadly Venetian in origin, and also called Istrian–Venetian. If I had asked my father, he would have said it was a variant called *Polesano* ('polesan'), the dialect of Italian Pola. My mother's dialect was also Venetian, from around Treviso, but had characteristics of the dialect of Monfalcone, where she spent most of her life before migrating. Once the newlyweds moved to Australia, she took on many of the words used in my father's dialect. That is what is special about dialect – it transforms slowly with circumstance, politics, time and place. It has idiosyncratic phrases or words that can be drilled down to a specific village, which can differ slightly from those used in the neighbouring village.

When you find someone who speaks your dialect, there is a strong connection, beyond the words and phrases. There are stories and memories, of family and community, a shared understanding of how to grasp reality. Once that is established, the discussion invariably leads us to our songs, the ones that we grew up hearing, sung in *dialetto*.

I never thought of our family and friends as musical, as they did not play musical instruments – but there was a lot of singing: at gatherings with friends, on picnics,

after Christmas lunch, even in some restaurants (if the owner was Italian and understood the importance of singing, when the sheer elation of being with your community overwhelms you). As written by Dino Leonardo Benussi in the magazine that my father subscribed to, *L'Arena di Pola*, Istrians always sang, in sadness and in joy, and it came as naturally to them as the beat of their heart. Their songs were nostalgic ones to be sung in company, reminders of the old country and a simpler life, creating a joyous chorus of voices and community.

You might call them folk songs, but we call them *canzoni vecie* ('old songs'), vignettes of everyday life with a good sprinkling of humour: 'La mula de Parenzo' is about a girl from the town of Parenzo, who had a shop that sold everything, except *bacalà* (salted cod); 'Ancora un litro de quel bon' is about drinking too much wine in the tavern, losing your house key and asking your wife to throw your mattress onto the street, as you're going to sleep out there.

Even though many of the older generation have left us, and we rarely have the opportunity to speak *dialetto* these days, we still sing the songs. They are part of the rich fabric of our lives, a reminder of those long gone.

Una canzon de una mula che gaveva
una botega che vendeva tuto fora
ch'el bacalà

The Istrian *bucaleta* or *bucalin* (in Italian, *boccale*) is a fat-bellied terracotta or ceramic jug, often decorated, with a handle and a spout. The spout is for pouring, of course – though traditionally not into a glass, but directly into your mouth. It was kept by the hearth in Istrian households, a symbol of sharing and community, in both good times and bad, when friends, family and neighbours would share wine, to celebrate or commiserate around the warming kitchen fire. The wine in the *bucaleta* could be spiced, with the addition of sugar, a bit of oil and black pepper, turning it into a type of mulled wine called *supa*.

Bread was the usual accompaniment to the contents of the *bucaleta*, but in festive times, it might be dark ring-shaped biscuits laced with nuts and spices. Domenico Rismondo, in his 1937 book *Dignano d'Istria, nei ricordi*, describes times of celebrations in Dignano/Vodnjan, when family and friends would be welcomed into the home, and in the colder months would huddle around the hearth, sharing a warmed *bucaleta* of red wine and spiced biscuits called *parpagnachi*.

Although we don't share jugs of wine in the same way now (the sentiment of conviviality can be just as strong if you drink from individual glasses), the idea of a warm and welcoming space in winter for those you are close to, sharing food and wine, is just as lovely. *Parpagnachi* are not too sweet, densely chewy, and have a wintery blend of warming spices that goes so well with red wine. I adore the texture, but be aware that as they do not contain butter, they are not crisp and flaky like your usual biscuit. It is purely optional for you to break them into pieces and dip them in the wine, like I do.

Spiced ring biscuits with cocoa & honey
(Parpagnachi)

Makes about 20

260 g (¾ cup) honey

175 g (1½ cups) walnut pieces

75 g (½ cup) almonds

250 g (1⅔ cups) plain (all-purpose) flour, plus extra if needed

20 g (¾ oz) caster (superfine) sugar

2 tablespoons Dutch (unsweetened) cocoa powder

zest of 1 small lemon

zest of 1 small orange

¼ teaspoon freshly grated nutmeg

1 teaspoon ground cinnamon

½ teaspoon freshly cracked black pepper

sea salt

1 tablespoon sunflower oil

½ teaspoon balsamic vinegar

icing (confectioners') sugar, for dusting (optional)

Preheat the oven to 150°C (300°F) fan-forced. Line a baking tray with baking paper.

Warm the honey in a small saucepan over very low heat until it is almost boiling (this will take about 10 minutes).

Finely chop the walnuts and almonds. (You could also use a food processor – but process the walnuts and almonds separately, as walnuts are much softer than almonds.) You don't want the nuts to be made into a flour; you should still see small pieces.

Place the chopped nuts in a large bowl together with the flour, caster sugar, cocoa powder, lemon and orange zest, spices and a pinch of salt. Stir briefly so that the mixture is homogenous.

Next, add the oil and vinegar, stir, then make a well in the centre. Pour the hot molten honey into the well, mixing with a spoon, then when cool enough, with your hands, working fairly quickly until a slightly sticky dough forms. As the honey cools, the dough will become firmer.

Break off plum-sized balls of dough, about 40 g (1½ oz) each, and roll into sausages about 12 cm (4¾ in) long. If they are too sticky, roll them on a lightly floured surface. Bring the two ends of a sausage together to make a ring. Place on your baking tray. Repeat until you have shaped all the biscuits.

Bake for 18 minutes, or for 15 minutes if you prefer a softer and chewier biscuit. The biscuits will still seem a bit soft when you take them out of the oven, but they will firm up as they cool. Don't be tempted to cook them any longer, as they will become very hard.

Transfer to a wire rack to cool. They should be eaten once they have cooled completely, and will taste even better the next day.

Dust with icing sugar before serving, if you like.

The biscuits will keep in an airtight container for several weeks.

Sauces, preserves & infusions

Salse, conserve e infusioni

Ajvar is a brilliantly coloured orange–red sauce found throughout Baltic countries. It has worked its way into Istria in more recent times and is now common on supermarket shelves. When I looked at the ingredients, I was surprised to learn that it contains eggplant (aubergine) as well as red capsicum (bell pepper). Before I knew this crucial fact, I had made up my own version, with roasted peppers, garlic and tomato passata, and now I like my version better. Adding red wine vinegar once it has cooled down balances the richness of the roasted peppers and the sweetness of the tomatoes.

This sauce goes well with grilled meats, vegetables, pies and even on pasta. I also use it as a base in which to cook stuffed banana peppers (page 117). I have been known to eat it with bread, like a dip – and just by the spoonful, cold from the fridge.

Roasted pepper sauce
(Salsa di peperoni arrosti)

Makes just under 300 ml (10½ fl oz)

1 large red capsicum (bell pepper)
1 tablespoon extra virgin olive oil
1 garlic clove, chopped
400 ml (13½ fl oz) tomato passata (puréed tomatoes)
chilli flakes, to taste
sea salt
2–3 teaspoons red wine vinegar

Preheat the oven to 180°C (350°F) fan-forced.

Place the capsicum on a baking tray and roast in the oven for about 25 minutes, turning over after 15 minutes. The capsicum skin should be charred and have softened, and may have released some liquid.

Carefully place the capsicum in a heatproof bowl and cover with an upturned plate. After about 10 minutes, you should be able to peel off the skin and remove seeds and core of the capsicum. Do not rinse the flesh under water, just roughly chop.

Place a saucepan over medium heat and add the olive oil and garlic. Cook until fragrant, then add the roasted capsicum, passata, a good pinch of chilli flakes and 125 ml (½ cup) of water (especially if the passata is store-bought, as it is usually thicker than home-made versions). Simmer for about 20 minutes.

Leave to cool, then process with a hand-held blender. Season to taste with salt, then stir in the vinegar.

The sauce will keep in a sealed jar in the fridge for about 1 week.

Béchamel, sometimes called white sauce, occasionally gets a bad rap. If it is made from a packet, it can indeed be awful. But the home-made version has wonderful binding properties (think of a dollop mixed with a meaty ragù between sheets of pasta – lasagne would not be the same without it) and if you do not use too much, it is terrific. In this book it is a key ingredient for the crepe stack (page 106), crepe cannelloni (page 109) and pasta strudel with peas (page 90). Make sure you use good-quality full-cream milk and good-quality butter; some real nutmeg also gives it a wonderful flavour. You can also halve the quantity of this recipe.

Béchamel sauce
(Besciamella)

Makes about 550 ml (18½ fl oz)

500 ml (2 cups) milk
60 g (2 oz) unsalted butter
60 g (2 oz) plain (all-purpose) flour
¼ teaspoon freshly ground nutmeg
sea salt

Warm the milk in a saucepan over medium heat, to just below boiling point. Set aside.

Place the butter in a second saucepan – one that will eventually fit all the milk – over low heat. Once the butter melts, take it off the heat and add the flour, whisking vigorously by hand to dissolve any lumps. Return to the heat and cook for a few minutes, or until the mixture turns golden.

Slowly pour in the hot milk, whisking as you go, to ensure the flour and butter mixture blends evenly into the milk without it burning on the base of the pan. Once all the milk has been added, exchange the whisk for a heatproof spoon and cook over low heat, stirring continuously, for about 5 minutes, or until the béchamel thickens.

Remove from the heat. Add the nutmeg and a good pinch of salt, tasting to make sure it is salty enough. Set aside to cool.

Many recipes will tell you to cover the surface of the béchamel with plastic wrap so that the air does not form a crust on top. However, I no longer use plastic wrap in the kitchen, and I have found that stirring it occasionally as it cools and then storing it in the fridge in a sealed container works fine. It lasts up to 3 days if stored correctly.

A few years ago while walking through the outdoor marketplace in Pola/ Pula in May, I spied rows of concrete benches laden with seasonal fruit: apricots, strawberries and cherries. I bought a handful of the rather small cherries to nibble on while I walked, stopping to take the occasional photo. I was somewhat disappointed – they looked fresh, with green stalks and leaves attached, but they were soft and not that sweet, quite different from my understanding of cherries. It was the texture that baffled me more than anything. It was only later that I realised they were sour cherries – called *visciole* in Italian. They are typical of the Istrian peninsula and of course I had eaten them before, but in a jar labelled Morello cherries. Eating them fresh is more of an acquired taste, but they are just lovely preserved, in cakes, poured over ice cream or simply on their own.

Sun-preserved sour cherries
(Visciole sotto spirito, senza spirito)

Makes enough to almost fill a 1.5 litre (51 fl oz) jar

1.3 kg (2 lb 14 oz) sour cherries (weight with pips and stems)
420 g (15 oz) caster sugar
60 ml (¼ cup) grappa (optional)

Wash the cherries, pat dry and remove the pits with a cherry-pitter. You should have just over 1 kg (2 lb 3 oz) pitted cherries. If you have less (or more) than this, adjust the sugar proportionally.

Place a layer of cherries in the bottom of a 1.5 litre (51 fl oz) sterilised preserving jar, then scatter over a tablespoon of sugar. Add another layer of cherries and a bit more sugar. Repeat until all the cherries and sugar have been used up, making sure the final layer is sugar and leaving at least 2–3 cm (¾–1¼ in) of headspace at the top of the jar. Cover with a layer of wax-free baking paper, then loosely screw the lid on the jar. Repeat if using smaller jars.

Set the jar in a sunny place, making sure it gets plenty of summer sun; the heat from the sun will dissolve the sugar. Shake the jar every day or so.

After 20 days in the sun, if the sugar has completely dissolved and the cherries have risen to the surface, they are ready. If not, wait a few more days.

Open the jar and remove the baking paper. At this point you can add grappa, which not only helps preserve the fruit for longer, but gives the cherries a lovely – and for me at least – Istrian taste. You can, however, omit the grappa.

Seal with a tight-fitting lid and store in the fridge. The cherries will last for 6 months and are delicious served over ice cream or by themselves. The syrup is lovely, too.

Grappa is often called *acquavite* in Istria, meaning 'water of life'. It is a distillate made from the skins of grapes leftover from wine making. I am not sure of the legalities of it, but you can buy home-made bottles of excellent-quality grappa very cheaply from farmers all over Istria. It is used not only in recipes, but can also be enjoyed straight up, or added to espresso as a *caffè corretto*, or made into an infusion.

I have been to many lunches with Ksenija and her charming husband Tomiza, both at their home and in *konobe* (restaurants), and had infused grappa as an *aperitivo* – often more than one type in one sitting. Memorable ones include a sweet olive grappa at Miramar Restaurant in Pomer; a walnut grappa made by Ksenija's mother, Gianna, using unripe walnuts from the tree in her backyard; and a carob grappa at Ksenija's house in Pola/Pula, with whole carob pods in an amber-coloured liquid. Some of the ingredients are a bit hard to come by in large urban cities, however you should be able to find ingredients to make the two infusions opposite, even if you do not grow the ingredients yourself (or know someone who does).

Juniper berries can be purchased from most supermarkets already dried; however, if you do have a tree, they will need to be dried out first. Whole carob pods could be easily purchased from health food shops in Australia some 20 years ago, but are impossible to find now, even though they are grown here. I managed to get a good result using carob kibbles, which is the pod broken into pieces with the seeds removed. It doesn't, however, look nearly as nice as having several whole pods in your bottle. You should be able to buy carob kibbles from health food shops, or online, but if you can get whole dried carob pods, which are available in some countries, even better.

Grappa
(Acquavite)

Juniper-infused grappa
(Acquavite col ginepro)

Makes about 500 ml (17 fl oz)

500 ml (2 cups) grappa
50 g (1¾ oz) sugar
6 juniper berries

Place the ingredients in a clean bottle or large jar with a lid. Seal and shake to dissolve as much of the sugar as you can. Place in a warm spot out of direct sunlight for 21 days, shaking the bottle occasionally. I wrap my bottle in a dark cloth to make sure it stays dark. The heat should dissolve the sugar after the first few days.

After 21 days, strain the juniper berries through fine muslin (cheesecloth).

Pour the grappa into a bottle and store in a dark spot for another 21 days. Your grappa is now ready to enjoy.

Carob-infused grappa
(Acquavite con le carrube)

Makes about 500 ml (17 fl oz)

500 ml (2 cups) grappa
50 g (1¾ oz) sugar
50 g (1¾ oz) carob kibbles,
   or 3 carob pods

Place the ingredients in a clean bottle or large jar with a lid. Seal and shake to dissolve as much of the sugar as you can. Place in a warm spot out of direct sunlight for 21 days, shaking the bottle occasionally. I wrap my bottle in a dark cloth to make sure it stays dark. The heat should dissolve the sugar after the first few days.

After 21 days, strain the carob kibbles through fine muslin (cheesecloth). (If you have a whole pod, strain only if necessary, and keep the pod in the bottle.)

Pour the grappa into a bottle and store in a dark spot for another 21 days. Your grappa is now ready to enjoy.

Carob-infused grappa has a slight chocolate taste, and is really good in a *caffè corretto*, where an espresso cup of strong coffee is 'corrected' with grappa and sugar to taste.

The basics

Ricette di base

Meat and chicken broth form the basis of many dishes in Istrian cooking, especially soups and risotto. Marchesa Eta Polesini describes a *brodo finto* or 'pretend' stock, made with vegetables, to be used in a time when meat and chicken are in scarce supply. A good vegetable stock, rather than a stock (bouillon) cube, will add a depth of flavour that is completely natural and without additives. Eta's original recipe used cured pork fat, which a *buona massaia* (good home economist) always had as a cooking medium through the year, as a product of the annual slaughter of the pig. I imagine that in the 1930s, when her book was written, there were not many people who were vegetarian by choice, but by necessity. I like to use olive oil in place of the cured pork fat to make the stock fully vegetarian. The addition of dried porcini mushrooms gives the stock real depth.

You might choose to discard or compost the vegetables once they have contributed to the stock. You could also do what my father did: eat them at room temperature with salt and a good drizzle of extra virgin olive oil. You can also double the recipe and freeze the stock for use at a later date.

Really good vegetable stock
(Brodo finto di verdure)

Makes about 1.25 litres (43 fl oz)

1 small celeriac, about 250 g (9 oz), peeled and chopped
1 handful of celery leaves
5 g (⅛ oz) dried porcini mushrooms
½ teaspoon sea salt
1 brown onion
1 small carrot
1 small celery stalk
10 parsley stalks (reserve leaves for another purpose)
2 tablespoons extra virgin olive oil

Bring 1.5 litres (51 fl oz) of water to the boil in a large saucepan. Add the celeriac, celery leaves, dried mushrooms and salt. Cover and bring to a simmer.

In the meantime, peel the onion and cut into rough pieces; peel the carrot and slice into finger-width pieces; slice the celery stalk; and roughly chop the parsley stalks. Place the olive oil in a frying pan over medium heat. Add the onion, carrot, celery and chopped parsley stalks and cook for about 6 minutes, or until starting to soften and caramelise.

Toss the sautéed vegetables into the pan of simmering water and cook at a slow, steady boil for a further 20 minutes.

Strain the stock, and discard or compost the vegetables (or eat them as suggested above).

The vegetable stock is now ready to use. If not using immediately, it will keep in a lidded ceramic container in the fridge for just under a week, or can be frozen for several months.

Isola/Izola is an old fishing village in Slovenia, only 15 kilometres (9 miles) from the border of Italy if you follow the coast, and much less by boat. My cousin Erni lives there and it is the prettiest of towns, with its Venetian architecture and narrow laneways. Fish is always on the menu, simply grilled or cooked in a soupy tomato broth, usually served on a bed of soft polenta to soak up the sauce.

This recipe is from Iolanda de Vonderweid's book *Ricette triestine, istriane e dalmate, antiche e moderne*, and she calls it *polenta squisita all'isolana* ('exquisite/delicious polenta from Isola'). It is paler than other polenta, as it uses half white and half yellow polenta. You can generally find white polenta at specialty Italian food stores; if not, you can just use yellow polenta. Serve with a goulash, *brodetto* (fish stew, page 133), *useleti* (little meat rolls, page 122), *polpette* (meatballs, page 128) – or even, as Iolanda suggests, topped with melted butter and plenty of grated parmesan.

To make a simple polenta, use the same method below, but replace the milk with water. As a rule of thumb, the ratio for polenta to liquid is 1:4. The variations to the basic dish are many – you can replace the oil with butter (and double or triple the amount) for a richer dish, use your favourite home-made stock as the liquid, or add handfuls of grated parmesan into the actual polenta at the end.

Polenta 'Isola' style
(Polenta all'Isolana)

Serves 4

300 ml (10 fl oz) milk
125 g (4½ oz) yellow polenta
125 g (4½ oz) white polenta
1 tablespoon extra virgin
   olive oil
sea salt

Bring the milk and 700 ml (23½ fl oz) of water to the boil in a saucepan. Now add the polenta in a steady stream, whisking it in by hand as you shower it in. Add the olive oil, and salt to taste.

Once it comes back to a vigorous boil, reduce the heat so it is maintained at a steady simmer, and swap the whisk for a wooden spoon. You will need to stir fairly frequently, although not continuously, for 30–35 minutes, adding some boiling water if it becomes too thick, until the polenta has cooked through. It should be thick, but still easy to stir and of a pourable consistency. It will become harder as it cools.

My mother used to say that polenta is cooked when it lifts off the side of the pan and a crust forms on the side and base. I don't quite cook it for that long, only until it is creamy and no longer granular. Taste it to check. Season to taste with salt and serve immediately.

Called *njoki* in Croatian, gnocchi are a common feature on restaurant menus and in homes throughout Istria. They are essentially dumplings and can be made of old bread, ricotta or semolina – though the most common (and the most well known in Italian cooking) is the potato version.

There is a skill to making potato gnocchi at home, and a few key factors will determine the success (or otherwise) of your gnocchi. First, you need the right type of potatoes. Red or purple ones work well, especially if they are old and floury – the old dried-out ones at the back of the pantry with roots growing out of them are best! You want potatoes with a low water content.

Second, you need to cook them in a way that decreases the chance of them incorporating excess water. My mother always boiled them whole, but if you experiment and weigh them before and after boiling, you will see that they absorb water that way. Try roasting them whole, skin on, directly on an oven rack at 200°C (400°F) fan-forced for 30–60 minutes (the exact time depends on their size). If you weigh these, you will see that they have decreased in weight and lost water. This is a good thing!

Thirdly, don't work the dough too much, or leave it on the bench for a long time, as the gnocchi will absorb the flour and become soft/wet over time.

Simple potato gnocchi are delicious with many sauces (including the beef and pork goulash on page 120), as well as baked with cheese and truffles (page 77). Once you master those, you can then try variations such as black gnocchi (page 78), or potato dumplings stuffed with cherries (page 82).

Potato gnocchi
(Gnocchi di patate)

Serves 4

1 kg (2 lb 3 oz) potatoes for gnocchi (such as king edward, desiree or other red potatoes)
sea salt
1 small egg, lightly beaten
250 g (1⅔ cups) plain (all-purpose) flour, approximately, plus extra for dusting

Wash the potatoes clean of any dirt and pat dry. Place them whole directly on an oven rack and turn the oven to 200°C (400°F) fan-forced.

After about 30–60 minutes, when the potatoes are cooked through and pierce easily with a fork, cut them in half and scoop out the insides with a spoon. Discard the potato skins (or place them back in the oven and turn them into crisps).

Rice the potatoes using a potato ricer (if you have discs with different sized holes in them, use the one with the smallest holes). Alternatively you can use a potato masher, though the resulting gnocchi may not be as smooth.

Spread the riced potatoes out on a clean, unfloured work surface (if you pile them up, they will steam and form moisture). While still warm, sprinkle over salt to taste, followed by the egg, incorporating evenly with the tines of a fork.

Sprinkle with about 150 g (1 cup) of the flour, and incorporate that evenly, again with the tines of your fork. Use a pastry scraper, and eventually your hands, to bring the mixture together, adding more of the remaining flour as needed. The mixture should be soft, but hold its shape, and should not be sticky. Try not to overmix or knead. When you think the consistency is right, scrape the dough off your work surface.

Clean your work surface and dust with flour, then place the dough back in its original spot.

Bring a small saucepan of salted water to the boil, so you can test a few gnocchi before rolling them all out.

Cut narrow logs of dough, no more than 5 cm (2 in) thick. Roll each log into a thick sausage about 3–4 cm (1¼–1½ in) thick, then cut off pieces about 3–4 cm (1¼–1½ in) long. Toss them in some extra flour. Roll on the back of a fork (or a gnocchi board) if you like; the gnocchi will catch the sauce better, but this is not strictly necessary.

Test one or two gnocchi in the boiling salted water. They will take a few minutes to float, which indicates they are ready; they should not fall apart. Taste for salt and for texture. If they do fall apart, or they taste too much like potatoes, work in a bit of extra flour, up to the maximum of 250 g (1⅔ cups). If you need more flour than this, it is possible that your gnocchi will become quite tough – and it possibly means that your potatoes were too wet.

When you are happy with the taste and consistency of your test gnocchi, roll and cut out the remaining gnocchi. Place on a lightly floured surface and cover with a clean cloth. Hopefully your sauce will be ready, or close to ready, as the longer you wait, the softer your gnocchi will become.

Bring a large saucepan of salted water to the boil; a wider pan is better than a deeper one. Using a slotted spoon, carefully drop some gnocchi into the boiling water – it should be at a slow rolling boil, not a vigorous one. Do not overcrowd the pan, as the gnocchi are quick to cook in batches if needed. Have a slotted spoon ready to drain and lift out the gnocchi as they rise after a minute or two, indicating that they are cooked.

Gently toss the hot gnocchi straight into your favourite sauce and serve.

Pasta is a combination of flour and a wet ingredient, usually eggs. The eggs can be replaced with other wet ingredients such as water or wine, either partially or completely. This recipe makes a basic whole-egg pasta for two people – but you can easily double or triple the quantity. This book has several recipes that use egg pasta, or a variant, so follow the instructions below for the method, but use the actual recipe itself for the quantities.

I describe the method using a hand-cranked pasta machine, but it can be applied to a motorised one. You can also roll out pasta by hand without a machine (called *sfoglia* in Italian). If you have never done this before, I would suggest searching online for a video tutorial or finding someone who can teach you. It takes some practice – and a very long rolling pin!

Many cooks use regular flour for dusting their work surface, but I routinely use super-fine semolina (or semolina flour). Also, I use a large pasta board made from untreated wood, with a lip that locks into the edge of my bench, as I find it is very useful to contain the work area. You can find these in stores that stock specialty pasta-making equipment.

Egg pasta
(Pasta all'uovo)

Serves 2

200 g (1⅓ cups) '00' pasta flour
2 eggs
super-fine semolina or extra
   flour, for dusting

Place the flour on your work surface in a mound and make a well in the centre. Crack the eggs (or egg and other liquid, if using) into the well. Start whisking the liquid gently with the tines of a fork, incorporating a bit of flour at the same time. Keep whisking, making an ever-widening circle as you incorporate more flour. The mixture will eventually become too thick for you to use the fork, so start using your fingertips, working the wet ingredients into the dry ingredients until you have used up most of the flour and a ball of dough forms. You may need to add a bit of water/flour to get the right consistency.

Knead for about 10 minutes, or until the dough is smooth and elastic. Place on a plate, cover with an upturned bowl and allow to rest for at least 30 minutes.

After your dough has rested, dust your work surface with semolina. Cut off half the dough and keep the rest covered.

Roll out the dough portion with a rolling pin until it is thin enough to go through the widest setting of your pasta machine. Thread it through the rollers of the machine, turning the handle to make the rollers move. Allow the pasta sheet to drop from the machine. Fold the thinned sheet in half, dust it with semolina if it is sticky, and give it a quarter turn, before threading it through the machine again. The quarter turn means that the pasta is going through the machine in a different direction and is essentially being kneaded. As you continue to fold, roll and turn the dough, the gluten will start to work, and it will become firmer and smoother. Repeat as many times as needed to make the dough lose much of its stretch (usually five or six times) and look somewhat glossy. Try to keep the dough in a rectangular shape, especially at the end of this process; you may need to use the rolling pin to help you shape it.

Once the dough has become firm and glossy, start turning the dial of the machine so the rollers are closer together, rolling the dough thinner each time. You no longer need to give the dough a quarter turn, and you will only need to roll it once through each setting. Dust the pasta sheets with semolina if the dough sticks to the machine as it goes through.

Repeat until your pasta is the desired thickness, then repeat with the other portion of dough. The sheets can be used in lasagne, or cut to your desired shape. Most hand-cranked pasta machines have an attachment that makes ribbon-like fettuccine, which is the simplest shape to make, and needs no additional equipment.

Dust your finished pasta with super-fine semolina, to help stop the pasta shapes or sheets sticking to each other (which happens more if you stack the pasta sheets or shapes in a pile).

Fresh pasta dries out quickly, so it is best covered with a clean tea towel (at room temperature) and used within several hours of being made. You could also store it in a cool spot, such as the fridge, for up to a day, well dusted with super-fine semolina, and in a single layer – preferably in a wide (not tall) sealed container.

At home we always called thin crepes *palacinche*, though some Italian–Istrians call them *amleti* or *omlet*, and Italians call them *crespelle*. As Sundays were special days, Mamma would cook a festive lunch, often a couple of courses – home-made pasta, a meat and a cake for dessert. Come dinnertime, we didn't want much, and that is when *palacinche* were offered. Grabbing a thin sandy-coloured round from the top of the stack, we would squeeze a cut lemon, catch the seeds with our fingers and let the juice flow between them onto the crêpe, which we would then dust with sugar. We would roll it up into a cigar, lemon juice spilling from the end as we bit into it, a lovely balance of sour and sweet. The *palacinche* Mamma made did not have sugar, so they were sometimes turned into a fancy savoury dish: a stuffing made with ricotta, spinach and parmesan would be spooned onto one edge of the crepe, which would be rolled up and placed on a baking tray next to other similarly prepared rolls, ready to be popped into the oven.

This base recipe is used for two other savoury dishes: Crepe cannelloni with radicchio and blue cheese (page 109) and Crepe stack with spinach, ham and blue cheese (page 106).

Savoury crepes
(Palacinche)

Makes 10–12

3 eggs
500 ml (2 cups) milk
225 g (1½ cups) plain (all-
   purpose) flour
sea salt
15–25 g (½–1 oz) unsalted butter

Whisk the eggs with the milk in a large jug and set aside.

Place the flour and a good pinch of salt in a large bowl. Pour in about half the liquid, whisking as you go, then pour in the rest of the liquid and whisk until smooth. Set aside for about 30 minutes in a cool spot.

Place a 21–23 cm (8¼–9 in) non-stick frying pan over medium heat. Add 1 teaspoon of the butter and swirl it around the pan to melt. Add a generous 60 ml (¼ cup) of batter, swirling it quickly so it evenly coats the surface, with just a small space at the edge so you can lift it up when you need to flip it over.

It should take about 1 minute for the crepe to turn golden and the edge to lift slightly. Flip it over using a spatula or tongs and continue to cook for 30–40 seconds until cooked through. Place on a warmed plate and repeat with the remaining batter, adding a bit more butter when needed.

Use in savoury recipes, or serve rolled up or folded with your favourite jam, or sprinkled with sugar and drizzled with freshly squeezed lemon juice.

The crepes can easily be made 24 hours in advance and kept covered in the fridge. To reheat, stack five crepes on a plate, cover loosely with baking paper and microwave for about 1 minute, until warmed through.

My friend Adriana is a ceramicist and lives in the hills on the outskirts of Melbourne. Her family is from Santa Domenica/Labinci. We bonded over our memories of food cooked in the family home and exchanges in our shared dialect, mainly about food: *'Orca che bon!'* ('Jeez that looks good!'), *'brava picia'* ('good little girl'), and describing our mum's gingham *'traversa'* (apron).

Adriana has a book with her mother, Lina's, handwritten recipes, and she shared her version of *palacinche* with me. And of course there are always stories that come with recipes. Adriana tells me that she phoned her mother on her honeymoon to get this recipe for *palacinche*, which she made for her brand-new husband (probably making him even happier he had married Adriana). She tells me they would eat them with apricot jam, which her mamma Lina would make with apricots from the tree in the backyard of the family home. Once the house was sold, and no longer having access to the apricots of her childhood, Adriana returned to the house by the sea, snuck into the backyard and took a cutting from the tree. She successfully grafted it to her own tree, and last year that new branch bore three of the sweetest fruit.

This recipe makes a delightfully fragrant version of *palacinche*, with citrus zests and white wine. If you do not want to use wine, replace it with extra milk, but it does add an extra depth. You can serve Lina's *palacinche* simply with apricot jam, just like Adriana did on her honeymoon – or else make them into a fancier dessert and serve them with cherries and ice cream, like I do on page 203.

Lina's crepes
(Palacinche di mamma Lina)

Makes 8

2 eggs
40 g (1½ oz) caster sugar
zest of ½ small orange
zest of ½ small lemon
250 ml (1 cup) milk
30 ml (1 fl oz) white wine
   (sweeter is better)
120 g (4½ oz) plain (all-purpose)
   flour
sea salt
10–15 g (¼–½ oz) unsalted butter

Hand-whisk the eggs with the sugar until well combined. Next add the zests, the milk and the wine and whisk again for about a minute.

Place the flour and a good pinch of salt in a large bowl. Pour in about half the liquid, whisking as you go, then pour in the rest of the liquid and whisk until smooth. Set aside for about 30 minutes in a cool spot.

Place a 21–23 cm (8¼–9 in) non-stick frying pan over medium heat. Add 1 teaspoon of the butter and swirl it around the pan to melt. Add a generous 60 ml (¼ cup) of batter to the pan, swirling it quickly so it evenly coats the surface, with just a small space at the edge so you can lift it up when you need to flip it over.

It should take about 1 minute for the crepe to turn golden and the edge to lift slightly. Flip it over using a spatula or tongs and continue to cook for 30–40 seconds until cooked through. Place on a warmed plate, covered if needed, and repeat with the remaining batter, adding a bit more butter when needed, but you shouldn't need a lot if the pan is non-stick.

If you are like Adriana, you will eat these rolled up with your favourite jam – perhaps home-made apricot jam.

The crepes can easily be made 24 hours in advance and kept covered in the fridge. To reheat, stack five crepes on a plate, cover loosely with baking paper and microwave for about 1 minute, until warmed through.

KITCHEN NOTES

I hope these kitchen notes help you make the recipes in this book in a way that is true to how I make them in my home. Some of the ingredients, or their use, may not seem very Italian – but that is the beauty of the food of the people of Istria, where communities, traditions and ingredients have blended over the centuries to give some of the recipes a more central European feel. Navigating these notes will, I hope, help you on your way.

Flour – I routinely use unbleached flour, organic where possible. If you only have space for two wheat flours in your pantry, I would suggest that plain (all-purpose) flour and super-fine semolina (used mainly for dusting fresh pasta) will cover most purposes. I also have finely milled ('00') soft wheat flour (to make thin pasta dough for ravioli), spelt flour (which imparts a lovely nuttiness), and baker's flour (for breads or longer proofing times). Using these specialty flours is not essential, but adds a nice touch in terms of taste or texture to the final product.

Eggs – The eggs used in this book are large – approximately 60 g (2 oz) – unless otherwise specified. I always buy organic eggs, laid by happy chickens that are allowed to roam on larger areas of land with access to daylight. I keep the eggs in the fridge, but bring them to room temperature before I use them.

Ovens and baking – Ovens vary greatly, with hot and cold pockets within the oven itself. It is important to know your oven and, with experience, you can understand by smell and appearance if a dish is cooking too slowly or too quickly. Furthermore, the temperature gauge on the oven panel can, over time, become less accurate, running hotter or colder than the temperature is set at. I tend to use a separate oven thermometer in the middle rack of my oven to confirm the temperature. Unless specified in the recipe, I use a fan-forced oven setting.

Grappa-soaked sultanas (golden raisins) – Like my mother did, I keep a jar of these in the fridge, as I use them often for making sweets. I use organic sultanas, which you can find in the organic section of your supermarket. Check the ingredients on the packet, and make sure vegetable oil has not been added (which is sometimes used so that the dried fruit separates more easily). Place the dried fruit in a small clean jar, top with grappa – a less expensive variety is fine – and screw the top on. The sultanas swell as they absorb liquid, so check every now and then that you have added enough grappa, and push the sultanas down gently with the back of a clean teaspoon to keep them immersed. If they are not covered by grappa, they are still fine to use (the high alcohol content of grappa preserves them), but the sugar can sometimes crystallise. Once you use up all the sultanas, you can reuse the grappa for soaking more sultanas in – or add a splash of the grappa to your coffee, like I do! A jar kept in the fridge lasts for many months.

Olive oil – I routinely use extra-virgin olive oil – a less expensive one for cooking with, and the best I can afford for using raw when finishing or drizzling over a dish, and dressing salads. Those in the know will tell you that the best-quality olive oil has a low acidity level and a particular pepperiness (*'pizzico'*). Price is usually a very good indicator of quality. When using raw olive oil, you should be guided by taste – what smells and tastes good to your palate. As a principle, olive oil should complement the dish, not overpower it. Istria has a long history of producing olive oil, since Roman times. Most is organic, made by small-batch producers, and of excellent quality, with green and fruity overtones.

Preserved anchovies – My pantry is never without a large jar of oil-preserved anchovies. I use anchovies as a base (together with garlic) for many otherwise vegetarian dishes, as well as seafood dishes. They add a rich saltiness, without that strong anchovy taste you get when you bite into one. They dissolve in the oil over time when cooking, and even people who say they do not like anchovies generally love the taste of the finished dish, often not realising that it contains anchovies. You do not need to store the jar in the fridge – as long as the anchovies remain covered in oil in the jar, they literally last for years in the pantry.

Ricotta – Made from the whey left over from cheese-making, ricotta can be made with milk from cows, sheep and, less commonly, water buffalo and goats. When first made, it is soft and creamy, and as more whey drains off, it becomes firmer and can be thickly sliced. It is versatile, mild-tasting and low in fat. I always have some in the fridge, and love eating it like my father did – for breakfast on toast with jam. It will usually last 4–5 days, if kept in a sealed container in the fridge. Discard it when it starts yellowing and has an unusual taste and smell.

Sauerkraut – There are many recipes online for making your own raw sauerkraut with cabbage, salt and a bit of magic created by lactic acid bacteria. Making your own is not very hard. It doesn't need much special equipment (a large lidded jar will do), and just a bit of patience (time). Jars of sauerkraut on supermarket shelves, unless labelled 'raw', have been heat treated and often contain additives. I tend to use store-bought jars for when I am cooking (bean soups or pork goulash), and enjoy the home-made raw version straight from the fridge.

Tomatoes – There is nothing quite as lovely as eating vegetables when they are in season, ripened in the sunshine or in the climate in which they grow naturally. This is especially true for tomatoes, which are at their best in late summer, and usually tasteless the rest of the year. Tinned plum or San Marzano tomatoes make a good substitute in many saucy dishes. A good brand will be naturally sweet – made from tomatoes that were ripened on the vine and processed shortly after picking. These tend to be the more expensive ones. If you use less expensive brands, you may need to add a pinch of sugar to the sauce or dish you are making, to lift the dish and give back the natural sun-ripened tomato sweetness.

Vinegar – Acidity in the form of vinegar adds a welcome balancing or brightening element to a dish, in particular one involving fatty or rich foods. It is also essential – at least for me – in a salad dressing. Vinegar is made by the fermentation of sugars into alcohol, which in turn ferment into an acidic liquid by way of acetic acid bacteria. The best vinegars are naturally (rather than chemically) fermented, and some, such as traditional balsamic vinegar, involve lengthy ageing processes. I always have the following in my pantry: red wine vinegar, white wine vinegar, regular balsamic vinegar and an aged balsamic vinegar.

SPICES

Where possible, I grind my own spices from seeds using a heavy mortar and pestle. I usually have the following in my spice cupboard when making Istrian food: caraway seeds, anise seeds, cumin seeds, black peppercorns, ground cinnamon, sweet Hungarian paprika, hot paprika, mild smoked paprika and whole nutmeg.

Aniseed or anise, not to be confused with star anise, is more commonly used in Italian cooking. It is sweet and aromatic, with liquorice overtones and is often used in desserts or liqueurs.

Caraway is frequently used in Central and Eastern European cooking. It has a warm taste, with overtones of fennel, and goes well with cheese and cabbage (especially sauerkraut).

Cumin has a slightly smoky taste that pairs well with paprika. Although we often associate it with Indian or Middle Eastern cooking, it is also found in some Germanic dishes.

Fennel seeds have a taste that is somewhere between aniseed and caraway, and can occasionally be used as a substitute for either spice.

Paprika is a red/brown/orange-coloured spice made of dried capsicums (bell peppers). There are many varieties ranging from mild to hot, sweet to smoky. The name on the label will usually describe which one it is. If the label reads only 'paprika', you can assume that it is sweet/very mild, and not smoked. Some are labelled with countries, specifically Hungary and Spain – though the label may just say it is made there. Hungarian paprika is mostly sweet, and there are eight varieties, which vary in heat. Spanish paprika (also called *pimentón*) is mostly smoked, with three levels of heat. At its sweetest, paprika adds colour and very little heat, and is a little bitter and fruity. Smoky paprika adds smokiness to a dish, not heat.

ABOUT THE AUTHOR

Paola was born in Melbourne, Australia. Her parents migrated from north-east Italy to Melbourne in 1950. Paola grew up in a family where the growing of food, the gathering of friends and shared meals were at its heart.

Paola's father, Nello, was known to frequently remind the family at the dinner table that 'the food you are eating was growing a few hours ago'. Nello never cooked but he had an enviable fruit and vegetable garden and loved the meals that Paola's mother, Livia, laid out on the table: rich bean soups, stuffed artichokes and fish *brodetto* (stew) with polenta, all of them reminders of their home on the Adriatic coast. They shared meals with the small Italian community they were part of and it was here that memories were shared and made. Food is not just a recipe, it is a story of the ingredients, of their provenance, of the person who made it and of their community.

Paola is a dentist by profession but long ago realised that what mattered most to her was food, cooking and its link to her family and their homeland. She established the award-winning blog 'Italy on my mind', where she shares recipes, stories of family and photos. Paola also runs a cooking school from her home in Melbourne and has run residential cooking workshops at the Anna Tasca Lanza Cooking School in Sicily, and food and wine tours of the Adriatic coast of Puglia and of Trieste and its surrounds. She discovered a passion for photography along the way and her Instagram account '@italyonmymind' is full of images of Italy and its food.

Paola has written, styled and photographed two cookbooks: *Italian Street Food* (2016) and *Adriatico: Recipes and stories from Italy's Adriatic Coast* (2018).

Istria: Recipes & stories from the hidden heart of Italy, Slovenia & Croatia is her third cookbook.

WITH THANKS & GRATITUDE

This book is for my father, Nello Martino Bacchia, and all the other *istriani* in Australia and around the world, those who left Istria and those who are still there. I owe so much of who I am to you, the land of your birth and of our ancestors, and the Adriatic Sea that surrounds it.

Thank you to the *istriani* who generously shared their stories, recipes and photos: Gemma, Margaret and Franca; Jolanda and Samantha; Tamara and Erminio; Ksenija and Gianna; Tara; Jenny; Adriana; and to my big sister Barbara (Babi) for many of the childhood memories of our family home and of our Istrian friends who are no longer with us.

Thank you to Vanessa and Barbara for testing recipes; and to my husband, Mark, for tasting every dish multiple times and being my sounding board for stories, recipes and so much more.

Thank you to Gabriella for my portrait; our shared love of Istria will always connect us.

Thank you to Ben and Adrian for the use of your beautiful home for some of the food photos.

Thank you to Claire for not only lending me your house and garden for photos but providing feedback whenever I requested it.

Eternal love to and gratitude for my mamma Livia who left us while I was writing this book; she was the taste-tester for many of the cakes and she would say *che bon che xe Paoletta*. I miss you every day, Mamma.

A huge thank you to Paul McNally at Smith Street Books for the opportunity to make a third cookbook, and the creative freedom to take it where I wanted it to go; to Lucy Heaver for expertly crafting it into the book you have in your hands; to Vanessa Masci for the evocative and beautiful design; to Katri Hilden for carefully editing my words; to Heather Menzies for typesetting; Helena Holmgren for indexing; and Ariana Klepac for proofreading.

Finally, Thank you to Rachel, for your quote and your love of stories and recipes.

BOOKS I HAVE USED FOR INSPIRATION

Lidia Bastianich and Jay Jacobs, *La Cucina di Lidia; Recipes and Memories from Italy's Adriatic Coast,* Broadway, New York (1990)

Aulo Crisma, *Parenzo: Gente, Luoghi, Memoria,* Centro di Produzione Multimediate, Milan (2012)

Iolanda de Vonderweid, *Ricette triestine, istriane e dalmate antiche e moderne,* Lint Editoriale, Trieste (1972–2015)

Mady Fast, *La Cucina Istriana, Storie e Ricette,* Franco Muzzio Editore, Padina (1990)

Francesco Gottardi, *Come Mangiavamo a Fiume, nell'Imperial Regia Cucina Asburgica e nelle Zone Limitrofe della Venezia Giulia,* AG Edizioni, Treviso (2005)

Vesna Guštin Grilanc, *Xe più Giorni che Luganighe; Cibi, Tradizioni, Costumi del Carso e del Circondario Triestino,* Edizioni della Laguna, Mariano de Fruili (1998)

Guido Miglia, *Istria: I Sentieri Della Memoria,* Unione degli Istriani, Trieste (1990)

Marchesa Eta Polesini, *Cosa Preparo per i Miei Ospiti: Pesci e Carni,* Casa Editrice A. Corticelli, Milan (1934)

Marchesa Eta Polesini, *Cosa Preparo per i Miei Ospiti: Antipasti,* Casa Editrice A. Corticelli, Milan (1934)

Marchesa Eta Polesini, *Cosa Preparo per i Miei Ospiti: Minestre, Erbaggi, Legumi,* Casa Editrice A. Corticelli, Milan (1935)

Marchesa Eta Polesini, *Cosa Preparo per i Miei Ospiti: Dolci da thè,* Casa Editrice A. Corticelli, Milan (1935)

Caterina Prato, *Manuale di Cucina per Principianti e per Cuoche Già Pratiche,* Schimpff, Trieste (1893)

Domenico Rismondo, *Dignano d'Istria, nei Ricordi,* Bagnacavallo, Ravenna (1937)

Maria Stelvio, *Cucina Triestina, XII edizione,* Editore Stabilimento Tipografico Nazionale, Trieste (1974)

Fulvio Tomizza, *Trilogia Istriana,* Mondadori, Milan (1967)

Anna Vascotto, *Ricette tradizionali dell'Istria e Quarnero,* Edizioni la libreria di Demetra, Verona (2000)

Edda Vidaz and Cesare Fonda, *L'Imperial Regia Cucina di Trieste, Pane, Primi Piatti e Stuzzichini Volume 1,* Luglio Editore, Trieste (2017)

INDEX

INDEX

INDEX

Published in 2021 by Smith Street Books
Naarm (Melbourne) | Australia
smithstreetbooks.com

ISBN: 978-1-922417-18-3

Photos of people in my stories
p. 25, Paola and Ksenija, Stoja, Pula, 1980; p. 41, Nello, Athens 1942; p. 53, Gemma and Mario, Melbourne 1957; p. 73, A gathering with friends: Bibo, Fide and others, Melbourne 1953; p. 127, Alice and Erminio, Italy 1947; p. 155, Nello and Livia, Monfalcone 1949; p. 183, Emma and Nives, Siana Forest, Pula 1939; p. 188, Mario, Monfalcone 1951; p. 205, Nello and Bibo, Melbourne 1952; p. 223, Picnic at Silvan Dam; Paolo, Emma, Antonietta, Ernesto, Stanco, Carolina, Barbara, Melbourne 1958.

Publisher: Paul McNally
Project editor: Lucy Heaver, Tusk studio
Editor: Katri Hilden
Cover designer: Vanessa Masci, Studio Terra
Design concept: Vanessa Masci, Studio Terra
Design layout: Heather Menzies, Studio31 Graphics
Photographer: Paola Bacchia, except pp. 61, 264 by Gabriella Favretto
Proofreader: Ariana Klepac
Indexer: Helena Holmgren

Printed & bound in China by C&C Offset Printing Co., Ltd.

Book 178
10 9 8 7 6 5 4